THE COME BACK CONGREGATION

INNOVATORS IN MINISTRY

THE COME BACK

CONGREGATION
New Life for a Troubled Ministry

RANDY FRAZEE
WITH LYLE E. SCHALLER

INNOVATORS IN MINISTRY

ABINGDON PRESS
Nashville

THE COMEBACK CONGREGATION:
NEW LIFE FOR A TROUBLED MINISTRY

Copyright © 1995 by Abingdon Press

This book is printed on acid-free, recycled paper.

Library of Congress Cataloging-in-Publication Data

Frazee, Randy.
    The comeback congregation : new life for a troubled ministry / Randy Frazee : edited by Lyle E. Schaller.
        P.   cm.   —(Innovators in ministry)
    Includes bibliographical references.
    ISBN 0-687-00620-1 (alk. paper)
        1. Church growth—Texas—Arlington—Case studies.   2. Pantego Bible Church (Arlington, Tex.)   3. Lay ministry—Texas—Arlington-Case studies.   4. 4. Arlington (Tex.)—Church history—20th century-Case studies.   I. Schaller, Lyle E.   II. Title.   III. Title: Comeback congregation.   IV. Series.
    BR560.A78F73   1995
    250'.9764'531—dc20   94-44331
                                                                                         CIP

95 96 97 98 99 00 01 02 03 04 — 10 9 8 7 6 5 4 3 2 1

MANUFACTURED IN THE UNITED STATES OF AMERICA

To the congregation of Pantego Bible Church:
Under God's leadership you have come back
and have also produced one very fulfilled pastor.
I love you very much.

The jacket cover contains a picture of a phoenix. The phoenix was the Greek name for the mythological bird that had a five-hundred-year life span. At the end of the five hundred years, the phoenix would build its own funeral pyre, on which it was consumed to ashes. Out of the ashes a new phoenix arose. Later, medieval Christian writers used the phoenix as a symbol of death and resurrection. *The Comeback Congregation* uses this symbol of the phoenix to signify the declining church coming back to life out of the ashes.

CONTENTS

Acknowledgments

I thank some very special people who have assisted me in the work of reviving Pantego Bible Church and for helping me tell the story through this book. First, I thank Jesus Christ, whose love for me motivates me without limits. Second, I thank my wife, who has been remarkably supportive of a husband whose calling in life is to invoke change. I thank God for my four children—Jennifer, David, Stephen, and Austin—who truly inspire me and are a visible reminder that it is important to "walk my talk" daily. I also want to thank my parents, my in-laws, Dr. Howard Hendricks, and Bob Buford for constantly encouraging me to press on and to make a difference with the "goods" God has given me. I thank the elders of Pantego Bible Church for developing a relationship of trust with me that has enabled all of this to work. They are crucial. I thank my staff, who have been instrumental in bringing ideas to the table and implementing those ideas successfully.

My secretary, Rita Ballow, is an amazing woman. She not only typed and retyped the manuscript of this book, but she also so gracefully and effectively manages my work. I could not have done this without her. I thank Kim Driggers, who used her gift to help me edit and rewrite the manuscript. I thank Aubrey Malphurs, chairman of the Department of Field Education at Dallas Theological Seminary, for allowing me to tag along at a lunch he had with Lyle Schaller. It was this meeting

ACKNOWLEDGMENTS

that launched the idea for the book. Lyle Schaller has been a mentor of mine for years through reading his works, as you will see in the pages of this book. I am grateful to him for encouraging me and believing in me. Finally, I thank Paul Franklyn and the people at Abingdon for the work they do and the opportunity for me to be a part of their team.

FOREWORD

The second biggest baby boom in American history occurred during the 1989–94 era when a total of 24.3 million babies were born. That compares to the 25.5 million babies born in the 1956–61 era, the peak years of the 1946–64 baby boom.

Where will the babies born in the 1989–94 era go to church in the year 2030? The safe answer, of course, is no one knows. A useful clue, however, is to look at where the babies born back during the peak of the biggest baby boom in American history are going to church. Where are the churchgoers born in the late 1950s to be found today?

First of all, they can be found in disproportionately large numbers in the congregations founded after 1960. The numerically growing religious traditions in the United States are those that launched large numbers of new congregations during the last third of the twentieth century. That generalization is consistent with American church history of both the nineteenth and twentieth centuries. The most effective single way to reach new generations is to plant new missions. The Bible warns against pouring old wine into new wineskins. That helps to explain why two-thirds to three-fourths of all congregations founded before 1960 are either on a plateau in size or shrinking in numbers. New missions represent a new wineskins' strategy.

The most highly visible exception to that generalization is the long-established congregation that relocated its meeting place to a new site. That decision was part of a larger strategy to make a fresh start at a new location to reach and serve a new constituency. These churches combined the assets of their accumulated institutional strength with a challenging vision and the freedom from tradition that is enjoyed by new missions to reach a new and unusually larger constituency. That also represents a new wineskins' strategy.

Where will the churchgoers born during the 1989–94 era be found? Like those from the 1956–61 generation, they probably will be worshiping in disproportionately large numbers in new congregations and in long-established churches that choose to make a fresh start in the new millennium at a new location as part of a larger strategy to reach a new constituency. A growing proportion will be members of multisite congregations that utilize facilities at two to fifty different locations.

Those three answers frequently provoke the response, "But that represents terrible stewardship! As Christian stewards of what God has given us, why do we have to invest so much of our resources in real estate? How can we justify that?"

One response to that plea is largely pragmatic: "We know how to do that. We know how to plant new missions that are designed to reach new generations. If we take advantage of what we know, we can achieve a 90 percent success rate in planting new missions that quickly will exceed three hundred in average worship attendance. We also know how to design a successful strategy for the congregation that decides to reach a new constituency by making a fresh start at a new location. What we don't know is how to revitalize long-established and tradition-bound congregations that are determined to keep doing yesterday over again. While planting new missions and encouraging existing churches to relocate is capital intensive, that may represent good stewardship if you use results rather than capital investments as the yardstick for evaluating the stewardship of resources."

That pragmatic response, however, is far from acceptable to those who insist, "But it shouldn't be that way! By now we should be able to help long-established churches design a strategy for reaching new generations."

This book is a response to that plea. This is NOT another book on church renewal or institutional revitalization. Those two words, *renewal* and *revitalization*, have created huge quantities of frustration among pastors and congregational leaders. One part of the explanation is they often were interpreted as relatively simple, easy, and painless undertakings. A second reason is they overlooked the central variable in the process of initiating planned change from within an organization. That key variable is widespread discontent with the status quo.

The big reason why many of the strategies for church renewal have produced more frustration than revitalization is they often were perceived as plans for renewal of the institution. The critical variable is to begin with the religious needs and the spiritual journeys of individuals. The revitalization and nurturing of the spiritual pilgrimages of people leads to the renewal of the institution.

How does one "renew" or "revitalize" a congregation in which most of the members are comfortable with the status quo? How does one renew the congregation in which the members enjoy growing older together, even if the price tag on that is shrinking numbers? How does one revitalize a congregation in which all institutional survival goals are widely supported and fully financed?

One answer to all three questions is that the traditional approaches to church renewal in those settings are usually rebuffed by a wall of denial, apathy, and indifference. A second answer is that the pastor-initiated strategy often results in the departure of that minister. A better answer is that the departure of the pastor is not the best beginning point.

The best answer is to postpone discussions of institutional renewal or revitalization and begin by designing a strategy for planned change that is initiated from within that congregation.

That requires skilled, informed, and wise leadership. The terms *renewal* and *revitalization* suggest to many people that all that is needed are a couple of patches on the old wineskins.

This book is about the need for new wineskins. It is not about the revitalization of a congregation—that is the by-product of a process that concentrates on the spiritual renewal, not of an institution, but of people.

This book is based on the assumption that most churchgoers are on a spiritual pilgrimage, but many have stopped by the side of the road to sit, relax, watch the parade pass by, and enjoy a passive spectator role. Many plan to arise and resume their own individual pilgrimage, but for now it is easier to sit and watch. This book explains how those spectators can be challenged to rejoin the march into tomorrow. This book uses the analogy of physical fitness to design a spiritual fitness plan for those who are now bored by that spectator role.

This book is the story of a "comeback congregation" that moved into a new era driven by a new vision of a new tomorrow.

What If It Works?

This book is about consequences. What if a numerically declining congregation is able to reverse that curve and begin to receive many more new members than it loses? Reversing that pattern of numerical decline is a result of change, but it also brings changes. This also can be seen in new missions that experience rapid numerical growth. The early model was organized around a two-point leadership axis of the pastor and volunteer leaders. Eventually new staff are added to the payroll. This can evolve into a disruptive triangle consisting of (1) founding pastor, (2) volunteer leaders, and (3) recently arrived program staff. Occasionally, the departure of a long-tenured founding pastor creates an identity crisis. "Our identity was in our pastor, and now the pastor has left, so who are we? What is our identity as a congregation?" As the leaders grope to create a new identity, many members find this is a convenient time to depart quietly. If the departure of that founding pastor creates a gridlock in the policy-making process, it is easy for the congregation to drift aimlessly. That encourages others to leave. If and when that pattern of numerical decline is reversed and a flood of newcomers begins to pour in, one consequence is the "strange face" syndrome. "I once knew nearly everyone and now half the people I see in church are complete strangers to me," grumbles an old-timer.

The level of complexity rises. "I used to be able to keep track of everything in my head," mutters a veteran leader, "but now I have to bring a thick file with me to board meetings to be able to know what people are talking about."

The other price tags on rapid numerical growth include (1) the capability to attract new people often exceeds the ability to assimilate them into the fellowship; (2) costs rise faster than receipts; (3) the internal self-image must be transformed from a community of members into a congregation of congregations of classes, choirs, cells, groups, circles, organizations, seekers, believers, disciples, leaders, followers, teachers, and friends; (4) the system of governance must be changed from centralized control to planning; and (5) the range of choices offered people must be enlarged.

Fans or Followers

This book is about leadership. One of the most common contemporary scenarios centers on the recently arrived minister who displays an attractive personality, is an excellent preacher, enjoys being with people, and is a loving and caring pastor. Within months this new pastor benefits from a rapidly growing fan club. "I joined this church in 1961, and our new minister is by far the best we've ever had," declares one old-timer. "The main reason we came here and are now members is because of the minister," explains a young couple who joined a few months after the arrival of the new pastor. A veteran leader brags to a colleague at work, "If you're unhappy with your minister, you ought to come to our church. Our pastor is a superb preacher, an excellent worship leader, and a wonderful model of a deeply committed Christian, and he truly loves everybody."

A couple of years later, after attending a ten-day workshop on evangelism, this enthusiastic pastor returns and eagerly suggests that the congregation implement a strategy designed to reach the unchurched. It includes a ten-hour training program for each of the forty volunteers required to implement the strategy. Ten of the new members and four long-tenured members sign up for the training program, but only six appear for the first session. The pastor is shocked, dismayed, and baffled. A few days later, one of the key leaders explains "Your plan has great merit, and I am convinced it has tremendous possibilities. The reason I could not come to that first training session is that it was scheduled the same night my service club meets. A lot of people here are concerned you're trying to move too fast. We've received nearly a hundred new members since you arrived, and many of our people feel we should concentrate on assimilating all of these new people before we try to reach larger numbers. We all appreciate your evangelistic zeal, but it might be better to take things one step at a time rather than try to move too fast."

A simple translation of that paragraph is, "Pastor, you have lots of fans here, but few followers. Be careful!"

This book is about the importance of followship. The most effective leaders are effective because they aggressively affirm the necessity of followship.

This book lifts up the value of a plan. Fans are attracted by magnetic personalities. Followers rally around challenges that are expressed in a plan with a detailed strategy.

Staffing for a New Era

This book is about team leadership. A key component of that leadership team obviously is a pastor who is able and willing to act as an initiating leader. An essential component of that team approach to planned change is a unified governing board that is supportive of change, but does not seek to micromanage the process. Trust is the cement that binds that relationship.

A second facet of the team approach to leadership is staffing. Whether it is volunteer leaders or part-time paid staff or full-time program people, the long-established congregation that is drifting in a goalless direction will not be able to design and implement a strategy for a new era without the leadership of a cohesive and unified leadership team.

A common example of this is the congregation with two or three adult classes composed largely of people who enjoy growing old together. Those classes will neither attract nor accommodate younger generations. The pastor and the volunteer leaders plus any paid specialized staff, must come up with a new design, if the adult Sunday school will be an attractive entry point for newcomers. The identification, enlistment, and training of volunteer leaders and teachers is an essential early stage in creating an adult learning community for the twenty-first century. This book includes an excellent case study on building and nurturing that network of volunteers.

Where will the babies born in the 1989–94 era worship in 2030? Like the babies born in the 1956–61 era, a disproportionately large number will be in the churches that (a) promise, "We'll help you raise your kids," and (b) offer the ministries necessary to fulfill that promise.

While far from easy to accomplish, the most attractive strategy for the long-established church to implement, if the goal is to reach younger generations, is to build the program required to fulfill that promise. This book offers a case study of how that can be accomplished. (See chapter 9.)

Why Choose This Model?

A few readers may question the wisdom of choosing an independent congregation, rather than a denominationally affiliated church, as the subject for a case study on innovation for reversing a period of numerical decline. Several arguments can be made to support that position. Independent churches do benefit from at least seven advantages that distinguish them from the long-established congregation with a close tie to a denominational system.

The most valuable is the absence of inherited denominational loyalties as a cohesive force that reinforces the ties of the individual member to that particular congregation. Instead of being able to rely on denominational loyalties for attracting new members, for retaining the allegiance of people who are moderately discontented with the status quo, the independent church must give greater weight to current performance. The absence of the sixth generation Presbyterians or the fifth generation Episcopalians or the fourth generation Methodists or the third generation Lutherans means that the independent church benefits from a more sensitive and faster feedback when performance drops below an acceptable level. In the denominationally affiliated church, many of the discontented, but denominationally loyal members may reduce their level of participation but they hang in hoping for a better day. In the independent congregation, the unhappy people are more likely to disappear completely. In all churches the members express their dissatisfaction with their feet and their pocketbooks. The independent churches benefit from the fact that for them this self-evaluation process is less ambiguous and faster.

A second advantage is locally generated goals are more attractive and more likely to serve as rallying points than those created in a distant headquarters committee meeting. This means that the leaders in the independent church can concentrate on formulating the goals required to turn that vision of a new tomorrow into reality. "Last year we doubled the number of single parent families we are serving," would be one example.

By contrast, the leaders at the denominationally affiliated church may reflect on the past with this evaluative statement. "While our Sunday school attendance continued to decline, we increased our funding of denominational agencies by 25 percent when our goal was only a 15 percent increase."

In workshops several pastors have challenged the order in which these advantages are ranked here. They place at the top of the list what this observer ranks third. This is the freedom the independent churches enjoy from those divisive pronouncements that come out of denominational conventions. One source of new members for many independent congregations is illustrated by this scenario.

The irate member rushes into the church office and shoves the morning newspaper in front of the pastor's face. "If this is what this denomination believes and teaches, this is not the church for me!" The newspaper article may describe a newly issued report by a study committee on human sexuality or a denominational statement on foreign policy or race or quota or abortion or education or war or some other divisive issue.

The pastor seeks to calm the angry parishioner by explaining, "This is only a study paper, it has not been adopted by our denomination. That is simply a statement to the churches. That does not mean we have to agree with it or support that position."

At best, these incidents are unneeded diversions. At worst they can be the source of a deep division with the congregation.

Fourth, when recruiting ministerial staff, the independent church can focus on character, Christian commitment, and competence. By contrast, the denominationally affiliated congregation may have to place a much greater weight on credentials and the criteria used by those who define the requirements for ministerial standing. In some traditions the denominational leaders assign pastors to churches.

Fifth, in seeking resources for ministry, the independent congregation usually enjoys the freedom to exploit all available resources, rather than depend on what is available from denominational headquarters. This list includes workshops, periodicals, curriculum materials, videotapes, computer software, strategies for change, seminar leaders, study books, and instructions on how a particular congregation should be organized.

Scores of volunteer leaders in independent churches who once belonged to a congregation with a close denominational affiliation contend that the number one advantage is the built-in trust of local leadership. They contrast this with the highly legalistic denominational systems that appear to be built on distrust of local leadership. In several traditions, the denomination has designed a system of congregational governance that must be followed by every congregation and/or it controls the system for ministerial placement and/or it assigns financial quotas for each congregation to meet and/or it defines the criteria for membership and/or it shapes the teaching ministries and/or it retains the authority to veto all major local real estate decisions and/or it acts as a regulatory body on many other matters. This "command control" system operated by officials in a distant headquarters appears to local leaders to represent distrust of the laity.

Finally, the independent churches have the freedom to choose and design their own support for outreach ministries and for worldwide evangelistic efforts. This makes it easier to make worldwide missions and/or local outreach efforts a central component of a renewal strategy.

These are seven of the reasons why the independent congregation often finds it easier to make a comeback after several years of numerical decline or to design and implement a strategy for a new era in ministry with new generations of people. That freedom is illustrated by this story of a comeback church. Congregations affiliated with a connectional type denomination such as The Presbyterian Church (U.S.A.) or the Christian Reformed Church or The United Methodist Church or the Evangelical Lutheran Church in America or the Free Methodist Church may encounter barriers in renewal that are not a problem for the independent churches. That denominational affiliation can be a major asset, especially for pastors, but it also can complicate the process of coming back from years of numerical decline.

From the What to the Why

Finally, this is a book about principles of innovation. This is not simply the story of how one congregation tripled its worship attendance in a few years. That story is here, but more important, the principles of how that was accomplished are identified and described. For example, in most congregations the adult Sunday school classes and the corporate worship of God are somewhere between unrelated and competitive. One part of the comeback strategy described here tells how the new Community Groups have become a central component of the larger strategy for ministry with growing believers.

Has the time come for your congregation to reverse years of numerical decline and make a comeback? If that is what God is calling your congregation to do, this is the book that will enable your leaders to formulate the principles that can turn your dreams into reality!

LYLE E. SCHALLER
Naperville, Illinois

INTRODUCTION

The 1991 movie hit *Sister Act* is a prime example of the drastic, yet positive revitalization of a dying church. Whoopi Goldberg plays the role of a Reno nightclub singer who dates a fast talking casino owner and drug dealer until she witnesses him murder someone. In an effort to protect "Dolores" (Whoopi Goldberg), a detective puts her under witness protection as "Sister Mary Clarence" in St. Catherine's, an inner-city convent in San Francisco. Only the Mother Superior knows her true identity. The convent is on the verge of closing down because it has been reduced to only a handful of parishioners.

In a place she sees as no less than a prison, Dolores takes over the choir. She throws tradition out the window and applies a very contemporary style to the music. She takes secular songs with lyrics such as, "nothing you can say can tear me away from *my guy*," and inserts *my God*. Somber hymns soon mimic upbeat radio tunes every Sunday morning. As Dolores slowly begins to experience the true worth and personal satisfaction from her assumed role, she also steps out of the convent and embraces true practical outreach. She begins to renovate the surroundings and to minister to the people on the streets through a day care and a food kitchen for the homeless. A fire is lit under the nuns and the Monsignor, and overnight the sanctuary is filled with people. To top it all off, the Pope hears about their work and decides to sit in on their service during his visit to the States.

Everyone's happy, right? Not exactly. The Mother Superior cannot accept the changes. Dolores's foot-stomping concerts are blasphemous to the Mother Superior, who believes she has corrupted the entire choir. But Dolores calls it like it is. Church is a drag, but with a little inspiration and innovation, she believes they can make it come alive, even for the downtrodden people.

This plot is not merely a farfetched Hollywood movie, but it captures the experience and energy of anyone who has attempted to revitalize a long-established church that is in decline. The purpose of this manuscript is to give the aspiring pastor an autobiographical account of the revitalization of a long-established congregation. Actually, a better term would be *revision*. Countless pastors have entered churches that lacked "vitality" and simply, through their charisma and hard work, were able to restore that church. Revisioning, however, involves revitalizing a congregation by refining its mission, by identifying the needs of a new constituency for a new era, and by translating that vision into specific goals. This can enable a congregation to reach a contemporary culture with the good news of Jesus Christ.

Pantego Bible Church is the story of how a long-established church was revisioned and revitalized. The story is told by a senior minister who entered a congregation in deep trouble, but felt with his whole heart before God that this is where he was supposed to be. Like Pilgrim, in Bunyan's famous *Pilgrim's Progress*, the church was in the "Slough of Despond," the mud pit that Pilgrim almost drowned in because of the heavy burden on his back. Things had reached the point that one member of the governing board broached the subject of selling the one hundred thousand plus square feet of facilities and moving into something smaller to reduce the financial burden. Was this a church that had never seen significant impact in its community and world? On the contrary, in the late 1950s, the 1960s and particularly the early 1970s, this church was caught up in the exhilaration of momentum. But the decade of the 1980s brought a devastating blow to this otherwise vibrant congregation for a variety of reasons. It was in 1990 that the board called me to take on the task of revitalizing this lighthouse for Christ. While the church is not experiencing growth in numbers as quickly as some of the recent church plant projects, it is, more important, experiencing the real solid growth and impact that comes through revitalization. Its sense of mission has been restored. The purpose here is to share the story of our journey over the last five years, and how we have seen this church come alive again. It can be done!

There are several reasons why such a story has value. First, most practitioners learn best from other practitioners. Most pastors do not want to hear theory in practical ministry apart from practice. One reason for the flood of pastors attending workshops on site at vital churches is that these same churches are actually growing and achieving a ministry vision others have only dreamed about. Pastors with vision want to know how to get there: "Show me somebody who's doing it and let me see what they've done and how they did it."

The second value has to do with hope. When you read this story, you will realize that ordinary men and women were involved in this work who had basically one thing going for them: "they had been with Jesus" (Acts 4:13 RSV). Your attitude should simply be, "If they did it, so can we." This account is designed to offer real encouragement to other pastors and church leaders; God *can* revitalize their congregations.

A word of caution must be given up front. What has been done by God at Pantego Bible Church (PBC), or any congregation that has experienced a surge of energy and renewal, is not necessarily the precise strategy another church with a different set of people, problems, resources, demographics, and opportunities should embrace. While a church can learn from another church's struggles and innovations, strategies and steps, each church must seek to adapt these ideas to their ministries in that location at the right time. So this work is not to be implemented without any thought given to what is appropriate for that particular congregation. Leadership is far more critical than a good idea or plan! Good ideas are great, but it is leadership that must implement the best ideas, at the best time, and in the best way possible for revitalization to become a reality.

The first chapter explains why church revisioning is a real challenge for pastors and church leaders as we move into the twenty-first century and why this really is a call for planned change.

The second chapter outlines in detail the steps we took to bring about revisioning. This gives the reader a basic under-standing of the history of the church, including its growth years and its decline and crisis. It concludes with an assessment of our results and where we are today.

The critical role of the change agent in the change process at Pantego Bible Church is the theme of the third chapter. It emphasizes the importance of the role of the pastor in the change process. Research shows that certain temperaments are more suited for the change agent's role in church revisioning. This chapter reveals the results of this study and how they matched assessments done on myself. Finally, it shares how God uses certain experiences to make me a more effective leader of change.

The fourth chapter explains how we organized PBC to not only rally around a new vision but also to lay the foundation for long-term innovation and effectiveness.

The fifth chapter will address the development of the mission statement and the role it has played in setting us on the right course. The unification and mobilization of our governing board is discussed in chapter 6. It not only covers the initial steps that were taken, but also the continual refining and focusing of the board over the last five years.

The seventh chapter describes the development and mobilization of the staff team with an explanation of how we developed and currently manage the staff to achieve our mission.

Chapters 8 and 9 outline how we approached the planning and implementation of our programs and describes our radically new approach to children's ministries.

The last chapter takes a look at the future. The comeback is complete. What will the next ten years look like? We have outlined four specific things we are dreaming about and why they are critical for our church as we approach the twenty-first century. How we approached the financing of this revisioning process will also be discussed.

CHAPTER 1

NEW WINE INTO OLD WINESKINS
The Opportunity for
Church Revisioning

COMEBACK CONCEPTS

1. Revitalizing a congregation becomes possible when the congregation perceives its crisis and decline.

2. Formula for Revisioning:

   A Perceived Crisis
   + Real Estate
   + People to Reach
   + The Right Leadership
   + God's Blessing
   _____
   = Church Revisioning

3. Most revitalization efforts will require casting a new vision for ministry rather than simply jump-starting the old ideas.

"And no one pours new wine into old wineskins. If he does, the new wine will burst the skins, the wine will run out and the wineskins will be ruined. No, new wine must be poured into new wineskins. And no one after drinking old wine wants the new, for he says, 'The old is better.' "

Luke 5:37-39

This passage has been used incorrectly by church leaders of this generation to show how futile it is to try to revitalize a long-established church. Even the novice theologian would conclude that Jesus' precise application was not aimed at the church, but rather at the unwillingness of the established religion, living under the Old Testament arrangement, to accept the new system of operations offered by Jesus Christ. However, the general principle seems to apply in concept with the changing and revisioning of long-established churches that have lost their edge and need to change but most likely will not. Resistance to change has done great damage to the growth of the church in the twentieth century. Lyle Schaller, in his book *Strategies for Change*, identifies a lag between societal change and the institutional response. The passage of time allows for changes that alter or eliminate the original purpose for existence, but the institution tends to cater to the old purpose until it disappears completely.[1]

Countless stories can be told of the battle scars and defeats that result when a minister attempts to change an institution catering to the old market. In his book *Where Do We Go from Here?* Ralph Neighbour tells of his twenty-five-year battle to revitalize seventy-five churches by installing a new relational evangelism strategy within these churches. While several of the churches were successful in their attempt at change, sadly he writes,

> By actual count, twenty-one of the seventy-five pastors who developed evangelistic Share groups have now been fired or were forced to resign by lay leaders who were totally threatened by the pastor's new outreach strategy. Their dismissals were directly related only to their attempts to revise the Program-Based Design structures and their challenges to the membership to get off the church campus and become involved in long-term faith sharing with their pagan neighbors. . . . When the twenty-first pastor called me from California to tell me his three-year-long struggle to develop relational church structures had ended in his forced resignation, I began to ask myself a serious ques-

tion: Can new wine be put into old skins? The answer is 'No!' Attempts at renewal don't work for one reason: our Lord told us over 2,000 years ago it could not be done. Every time we try to ignore His clear teaching, we fail. In retrospect, I could have saved myself 24 years of dreaming an impossible dream if I had taken His admonition literally. While I was trying to renew, He was shaping something brand new."[2]

As a result of countless experiences like this one, leaders started tiptoeing around the established church to get the job done. There was a large movement to start parachurch ministries (Young Life and Campus Crusade for Christ, for example) in the early 1950s and 1960s while the pace of church planting really took off in the 1970s. Church planting is still a powerful force today, and the results of these new organizations and churches are significant to the Body of Christ.

The Frozen Assets in the Established Church

While the parachurch and church planting endeavors have generally been successful, there is an empty feeling that comes over the Christian leader in considering the tremendous amount of money and time poured into thousands of existing churches that now sit almost empty.

Consider just the vast amount of real estate that has been developed in an estimated 350,000 Protestant churches in America. If we assume that the average established church has a conservative $250,000 invested into their facilities, you discover that the church of Jesus Christ has already invested $87.5 billion! To simply walk away from large parts of $87.5 billion in real estate is an example of poor stewardship. Though many have tried to revitalize some of these churches, they have found starting from scratch to be far more effective and less frustrating. I am forced by example to agree with this conclusion, but good stewardship forbids us to accept it as a given.

The Missing Ingredient

Lyle Schaller, in his work *Strategies for Change,* states that change and new ideas are on the offensive and can gain real momentum in a church or organization when that church or organization perceives they are in crisis. During a crisis, the influence of the proponents of change is increased, and the opponents of change are on the defensive. A crisis tends to open up the channels of communication by accelerating the speed of communication, by facilitating the opportunities for two-way communication, and by substantially altering the behavior of individuals.[3]

The question is, "Are there a number of established churches that perceive their crisis?" Many have known for years that the church was in a crisis. But there is a significant difference between having a crisis and knowing about it. Schaller writes, "There is usually a lag between the time when the period of crisis actually begins and when it is perceived. Until it is perceived, the behavioral responses will tend to follow the normal patterns."[4] If there are a substantial number of churches aware of their crisis, then the ministry of church revisioning is open with real opportunities for impact.

Win Arn's study demonstrates that **80 to 85 percent of established American churches are either on a plateau or in decline.**[5] As a result, Arn concludes that four of every five churches are being set up to either close their doors or face revisioning. This means that as many as 297,500 of the 350,000 churches today are being faced with these choices. Choosing to revision, given the right conditions, results in an exciting formula for real growth.

A Perceived Crisis (e.g., drop in attendance, contributions)
+ Real Estate
+ People to Reach
+ The Right Leadership
+ God's Blessing

= Church Revisioning

Sixty percent of Americans claim that they do not attend church on a regular basis.[6] However, actual behavior indicates that this number is probably much higher. A study by Kirk Hadaway and Penny Marler, published in the *American Sociological Review*, found that half the people who tell pollsters that they spend Sundays in church aren't telling the truth.[7] Only 20 percent of Protestants and 28 percent of Catholics show up on Sundays. These figures are based on actual head counts in selected churches, which were then compared with surveys of the same communities. The explanation for the discrepancy is that most people believe voting or going to church is a good thing to do and, when surveyed, often say they vote or go to church even when they don't. This means that there is still a need for these established churches to set their sights on outreach. However, without the right leadership and God's blessing, the first three ingredients will not produce revitalization.

Under these circumstances, church revisioning is not necessarily harder or more costly than church planting. It is different. Both have their unique set of problems. The question becomes, "Which set of problems do you want to live with?" Fortunately, with God's help and the right ingredients, we were able to make revitalization successful at Pantego Bible Church.

CHAPTER II

FROM CRISIS TO RECOVERY
A Brief History of
Pantego Bible Church

COMEBACK CONCEPTS

1. Turning around a congregation in a tailspin is a very difficult process that must be entered into only with a sense of a calling from God and your eyes open to the real challenge.
2. The revitalization process takes four to five years.
3. The revitalization process involves taking what you have left to build the corporate self-esteem of the congregation—a belief that they still have a contribution to make in society.

The Establishment of PBC

The Bible Church movement was created in the days following World War II out of the growing desire of people for churches where the teaching of the Bible was central to the church's ministries. There was a strong tendency among the more liberal churches to move away from the doctrinal positions for the authority, inspiration, infallibility, or inerrancy of the Bible. Hundreds of independent or nondenominational Bible churches were founded in response to this need. Today they have a combined worship attendance in North America of at least one million people on the typical weekend.

A small church was formed in the early 1900s called Pantego Community Church. But it wasn't until the early 1950s that a group of people ventured out to start a nondenominational Bible Church in the small but growing town of Arlington, Texas. They began by starting a Sunday school program for children. The town already had one church represented by each of the major denominations. These people felt a Bible church would meet a need for many people looking for solid Bible teaching. (There was a core group of families who were actually meeting together in the early 1930s under the unincorporated name, Pantego Community Church.) The leaders planned for this unique children's Sunday school program to ultimately reach the parents, thus providing the spark for a church to be officially founded. This did in fact take place, and the church was incorporated in 1956. The church started by using student pastors from Dallas Theological Seminary.

The Growth Years

In 1961, the first full-time pastor, who would spend the next twenty-five years at PBC, came on board. Three significant things took place that caused the church to grow. First, the senior minister was an effective leader for the times. Secondly, the Arlington community experienced explosive growth due to (1) the increase in several large businesses setting up offices or plants in the city, and (2) the "spill-over" growth from Dallas and Fort Worth. Finally, the Arlington community experienced tremendous economic growth from the 1960s through the early 1980s with the opening of the Dallas-Fort Worth Airport. The available resources allowed the church to build over one hundred thousand square feet of space, create a large program staff, and design programs to meet the needs of the people. As a result, the church grew from 250 people in worship in 1961 to over 1,300 in 1984 and 1985. The church earned the reputation for being the most successful church in the community. It was the talk of the town.

The Crisis

Today, if you talk to those who were in leadership during this time, they would agree that the crisis started developing in the mid to late 1970s. The church as a whole, however, did not know, understand, or recognize this developing crisis. According to church records, PBC began to experience a slight but steady decline. It is hard to say what precisely caused the crisis, but this is not relevant for our purposes. It is important to note, however, that the crisis did not involve a sexual scandal. The most prominent cause was a growing struggle the senior minister had with his large program staff. This is one of the most common price tags of rapid numerical growth. That shift from a pastor plus lay volunteer leadership team to a senior minister plus staff plus volunteer leaders often creates a disruptive triangle. It appears that no one was completely guilty or guiltless in the matter. These internal struggles in leadership were exposed and confronted in 1985 and ultimately led to the resignation of the senior minister in 1986.

The Decline

The church started to fall apart at the seams. People began to leave. For many people an attractive, natural, and predictable response to internal conflict is to walk away. Most adults tend to avoid both people and institutions who are perceived as going through an identity crisis. Consensus on direction was extremely difficult, if not impossible. The policy-making processes were gridlocked. As a result, the church went without a senior minister from 1986 to 1990. Worship service attendance plummeted from 1,300 to 425 during this period. Contributions to the General Fund dropped from $16,000 a week to $4,000 a week. Missions giving went from $400,000 a year to

$200,000 a year. The full-time twelve-member ministerial staff was disbanded, leaving only one hopeful after the whole ordeal. The church's reputation in the community and around the world was greatly damaged. Everyone concluded that Pantego Bible Church was a tragedy never to be revived, but God had another plan for this congregation.

After a two-year waiting period, which was undeniably used by God to strengthen my spiritual life and build me into a leader of change, I became the senior minister in February of 1990. The details of this process are discussed later. First, let's take stock of the environment with which we had to work.

What We Had Working Against Us

Two significant emerging realities were hard to overcome. First, PBC had a great deal of negative advertising spreading by "word of mouth" throughout the community. This image would take significant time to undo. Second, the remaining congregation was suffering from a low corporate self-esteem. It was questionable whether the members believed that revitalization was possible.

What We Had Working for Us

The crisis itself was probably the greatest factor working for us. Everyone in the church, from the governing board to the person in the pew, knew that things had to change. They were discontent with business as usual. This put change on the offensive for a brief window of opportunity. The timing was right to act on a positive vision for the 1990s and on into the twenty-first century.

We had several other positive elements working in favor of revitalization. Five specific realities helped us in our journey. First, in the four years without a senior minister and the loss of all the program staff, most of the old systems and ways of doing things naturally disappeared with them. This lapse of time enabled us to come in and develop new systems and procedures for the execution of our ministries without much resistance. Of particular significance was the elimination of most of the committee structures in the church. This was a small loss since they were ineffective in getting the job done. We were able to develop a more streamlined and less bureaucratic approach to ministry.

Second, we did a fairly extensive survey of all the churches in the Arlington area and discovered a large percentage of unchurched people that no one was reaching. As a matter of fact, our conservative estimate indicated that 74 percent of the 270,000 Arlington residents did not attend church. This figure magnified in significance when you consider that we are in the heart of the Bible Belt. Bible Churches have carried the unspoken notion that all the lost souls of the world are found overseas. This startling report gave our people a new sense of mission, not only to develop the believer, but to aggressively reach out to the "seeker."

Third, we had over one hundred thousand square feet of debt-free facilities, as well as ample off-street parking for substantial growth. Fourth, we carried a nondenominational label, which seems to have become more and more attractive to people who do not want to join churches entrenched in denominational tradition. Finally, we had a long-standing reputation for teaching the Bible.

In just four years worship attendance climbed from 425 to over 1,200. Our offerings increased at a rate of 20 to 25 percent each year. But the most exciting element is the environment of life change. An electricity exists within the walls again that may be stronger than it ever has been. How did that happen? That is the central theme of this book.

Listen to the letters of a few of our members on how they have responded to the change we have instituted. It can be positive!

The vision that God has given you for Pantego has had a positive impact in many people's lives. Otherwise the church would not be growing and people who had left would not be returning. Frank and I fall in that last category. We left Pantego about six years ago because there seemed to be a lack of vision and direction from the interim leadership. . . . Change affects people in different ways. Some people seem opposed to change of any type. If you believe that your current position is where God intends you to be; then I believe that the vision you have is God's vision for change in this church.

I know that I desire to be changed by God and have changed in many areas of my own life. My personal growth and ultimate yielding to His leading in many areas of church worship have come about as a result of trusting you and knowing that it isn't your plan for our church but God's plan revealed to us through you. While change isn't ever easy, as a whole I feel our church has tried hard to keep pace with all the changes. . . . I am behind you all the way.

Bill and I want to take this opportunity to tell you how we enjoy the direction the church is taking. We have been members since the early 1980s and were very fond of the previous Senior Minister. His departure and the months before you came to the church were very sad for us. However, since you have taken the helm, we feel that the church is making a very positive move forward. We both feel very positive about Pantego and look forward to being a part of its future.

CHAPTER III

CHANGE REQUIRES A CHANGE AGENT

COMEBACK CONCEPTS
1. The change agent is almost always the senior minister.
2. Certain people are better suited than others to successfully fulfill the role of a change agent.
3. God often tests the leaders of church revitalization before they come into their role to deepen their character and trust necessary to perform the duties required.

A change in personnel alone does not guarantee effective revitalization. There are so many other factors that come into play. However, revitalization without a change agent is difficult. For the church, this agent is almost always the senior minister. In studying both the Old Testament and the New Testament, notice a specific pattern to God's administration. A point person, who leads God's people toward the goal, is selected. Moses, Joshua, David, Peter, Paul (from the Bible), Martin Luther, and John Wesley (from the Reformation) are a few examples. If revitalization and revising is to occur, a point person must emerge.

The revitalization of Pantego Bible Church is no different. I had to face the decision to assume that role.

The Personality of the Change Agent

"Can anyone be a change agent?" "What does a change agent look like?" "Am I a change agent?" These were questions that swarmed around in my head in 1990. My gut instinct told me that my personality was one of a change agent, but only later did I come to discover why. Emphasizing the importance of a change agent, however, is not to imply that this is the greatest worker in God's kingdom (Matt. 20:20-28). A change agent is merely someone who comes into a long-established church and acts as the point person for revitalization. There are many other important roles in the church that must be fulfilled. Each of these roles requires a certain mix of gifts, temperament, and of course, a passion for the job.

Lyle Schaller has made several observations about the effective change agent from his vast experience as a parish consultant. In his book *Create Your Own Future!* Schaller writes, "One of the more highly visible methods of intervention in congregational life is the appearance of the skilled, persuasive, respected, influential, and effective leader who (a) has a vision of a new and different tomorrow, (b) can persuasively communicate that vision to others."[1] In another book, Schaller states that "revitalization as a movement requires certain types of leaders, who by temperament, are reformers, not revolutionaries, who are patient and able to accept a long-term view of the process of change, who view compromise as a useful tactic in that long-term process, and who are comfortable working within the existing structures of society."[2]

A more specific study was done by Robert Thomas, who used the *Biblical Personality Profile* developed by the Carlson Learning Center in Minneapolis. He studied churches that experienced little if any growth over a three-year period. He then followed those churches who hired a new senior minister. Those churches that grew were pastored by ministers who fell within the profile of the Persuader Pattern.[3] Carlson Learning Center provides this description of the Persuader Pattern.

Persuaders work with and through people. That is, they strive to do business in a friendly way while pushing forward to win their own objectives. Possessing an outgoing interest in people, Persuaders have the ability to gain the respect and confidence of various types of individuals. This ability is particularly helpful to Persuaders in winning positions of authority. In addition, they seek work assignments which provide opportunities to make them look good. Working with people, challenging assignments, variety of work and activities which require mobility provide the most favorable environment for Persuaders. However, they may be too optimistic about the results of projects and the potential of people. Persuaders also tend to overestimate their ability to change the behavior of others. While Persuaders seek freedom from routine and regimentation, they do need to be supplied with analytical data on a systematic basis. When they are alerted to the importance of "little things," adequate information helps them to control impulsiveness.[4]

I have taken the *Biblical Personality Profile* on four occasions and each time I came out a Persuader, so now I am convinced that church revitalization takes more than just good ideas. There are a number of good books on the market today that give a person very specific and powerful ideas for an innovative church. The difficulty is getting those ideas into play at the right time with a large group of discouraged people. Getting people to embrace ideas, try those ideas, and then upon initial success continue those ideas, is the difference between an idea and a positive step toward leadership in church revitalization. God seems to wire certain people for that role of Persuader (Rom. 12:3-8; 1 Cor. 12:12-31).

Ralph Mattson, the president and founder of the DOMA Institute (which specializes in organizational development and assessment technology), also did an assessment on our initial team at PBC in 1990. This study further confirmed why church revitalization is a match for me. Three of the areas that DOMA assesses are one's "energy," "destination," and "time." Energy defines what a person is pulled or pushed into; what energizes them. Destination defines that particular person's desired goal for themselves. Time essentially relates to how that person makes decisions. Here is how I was assessed in these three main areas:

Energy (Pull): Where something new can be developed and where order can be established.

This essentially means that as a persuader, I am pulled into situations where there is disorder and chaos. The persuader is motivated to come into an organization and develop a new strategy for effectiveness and then take great pains to see to it that the new order is actually established. If the people do not see the ineffectiveness of a particular area, I will start the process off by trying to bring the problem to the surface. So the intentional persuader is in one of two phases—either creating discontent for the status quo or organizing, structuring, directing, and enlisting for a new order.

Time: Sporadic

As a persuader, I make decisions and use my time differently according to the circumstance or phase at hand. While trying to create discontent for the status quo, my time is open and highly relational. If the need for change is perceived by the necessary group of people and it is time to act, my time becomes more closed and efficient.

Destination: Where you are critical to the success, where you have performed well as a result of thorough preparation and where you have been recognized for your value.

Essentially, my passion is to be a point person for change. Every morning, it is a struggle to downplay my passion to revitalize Pantego Bible Church in order to successfully perform my other essential roles of husband and father of four children. Other activities that don't directly tie into this project do not motivate me. In terms of job satisfaction, I couldn't be happier.

Many churches cannot make a comeback because they hire a person who has the proper educational background and looks the part, but this person does not have the temperament, gifts, and passion to do the job of a change agent. In many places of leadership I wouldn't fit, but church revitalization is my niche in the Body of Christ. Does this mean that a person who does not match the above assessment can't be effective in the revitalization process? It's hard to say, except that the descriptions and assessments that have shown up in successful change agents are consistent across the board. Many things we can't do, but God empowers others in his body to pick up the pieces where our gifts and talents fall short. In the Body of Christ, we all have equal value but different functions to perform (Eph. 4:16).

The Making of a Leader of Change

A change agent with the proper temperament for the job and the necessary academic degrees is still incomplete from God's perspective. God is also interested in the character and spiritual maturity of the leader. How does God achieve this in a willing vessel? You will be tested.

When Samuel went to Jesse's house to select a new king for Israel, Jesse did not even consider his youngest son, David. He was left out in the field to shepherd the sheep on the day his brothers were interviewed. Through Samuel's persistence, David was brought from the field and anointed as the next king of Israel. What happened next? David waited twelve more years before he was actually inaugurated as king! What did David do during those twelve years? Most of the time, he was running from King Saul. David was being refined for the job ahead of him.

On several matters I would not compare myself with King David, but I can relate to the process God used to prepare him for his job. In 1985, I came to Pantego Bible Church as a regular attendee. I was working with a parachurch organization that was based in Arlington, and the director attended the church. In 1986, the senior minister resigned. As the church started to decline slowly and go through its crisis, I began to teach an adult Sunday school class of about three dozen people born between 1950 and 1960. As the church continued its decline, this class grew to over one hundred in attendance.

In January of 1988, a member of the search committee approached me to put my name in for senior minister. At the time I was twenty-seven years old. After some thought, I really felt that this is what I was to do. After giving my response, the committee did not talk to me again until October. After a series of stressful events, I was finally presented to the congregation for affirmation in January of 1989. Due primarily to the unpurged membership list, many hostile people, who had left the church, returned to sway the vote. Many of the new people who were excited about the proposal on the table were not members and were thus unable to vote. I was the second person to fail to secure two-thirds of the congregation's vote. While I strongly sensed that this position was what God was calling me to do, I went back to my office the next Monday morning to continue my work in parachurch ministry. I knew that I had to leave the church to make room for a new senior minister without worry of my situation.

One week later, I received a call from some of the key leaders of the church. They asked me if I would serve on an interim team with two other individuals in the church, one a seminary professor, the other a missionary. They feared the church was going to lose the large group of younger adults who were deeply disappointed in the results of the congregational vote. After about two weeks of wrestling with my pride, I finally agreed that this would be best for the church and I took on the assignment. It was a humiliating but necessary experience.

In February of 1990, the leadership decided to bring my name before the congregation again and I was confirmed as the senior minister with an 86 percent approval. All of the people who did not attend the church were purged from the rolls. A strong emphasis was placed on getting the new people into membership. I am convinced that this two-year process was used by God to develop my character for the challenges that lay ahead.

While my time at Pantego has offered me many opportunities to experience humility, there is nothing like living with the sense that you are using your God given gifts to make a difference in people's lives. From time to time a member affirms you as a change agent as the following letter illustrates.

I thank the Lord for you. Your ministry and teaching have enriched my relationship with Jesus. I am at my spiritual best right now and know that the more I seek God the more He reveals His will to me.

I am also thankful for your leadership and vision. As a marketing strategist at American Airlines, I appreciate focus on core competencies and moving full steam ahead. I applaud your vision for the ministry of Pantego. It's exciting and thank you for including us at the ground level. The energy you spend to communicate so personally with us will pay mighty dividends, I am sure. I feel valued as a worker to be among the first to respond to many of your ideas. I am behind you all the way. I look forward to investing my gifts in the ministry of Pantego. Thanks again for making the tough decisions and helping us all make the most impact for Christ.

CHAPTER IV

THE MAGNA CHARTA
Liberating the Church to Innovate

COMEBACK CONCEPTS

1. A specific and targeted sense of direction must be outlined in writing by the senior minister in the first year.

2. The church board must adopt several values that are inbred into the life and culture of the church that set the ground rules for change and prevent the church from returning to the same position of decline and crisis in the years to come. That board must stand by the senior minister as he takes the hits for the changes made from these values.

3. It is critical to make tough decisions regarding the direction the church is going to take. A church in decline only has the strength and resources to be good at a few well-defined targets. The change agent must define this focus very early in the process of revitalization.

A Magna Charta is defined as a document that officially liberates a group of people by stating a new order guaranteeing certain rights and privileges. It was clear that the church was gridlocked and enslaved. Trying to develop a direction for the church that would please everyone would, in essence, end up offending everyone. We had to choose a direction; we could

---

not become all things to all people; we had to look at who we were trying to reach and could reach based on our circumstances and resources.

The decision about our direction was a simple one in light of the grim facts, but the change would be a hard pill to swallow for many. We knew we would be unable to galvanize the entire congregation initially, but if we could galvanize the governing board around a new mission, we could stand united against the storm we would inevitably face as a result of all the necessary changes. We all had to be on the same page when it came to the philosophy of ministry. We needed a solid base to go back to and measure our decisions against when times got tough. I needed accountability and assurance that the board members would not continue to change their mind in the midst of pressure from the congregation.

It was refreshing to read Lyle Schaller's book *Strategies for Change,* a practical how-to book that could actually help me evaluate and walk through the process of change. In this book, Schaller states twelve characteristics of an innovative organization. If these twelve characteristics were a part of the philosophical makeup of the leadership, ongoing change would not only be possible but encouraged.[1]

I decided at that point to draft a one-page document outlining these philosophical principles, as well as some additional necessary decisions, and take them to the governing board before taking the job. If the board was galvanized around this statement, we could move forward. If they were not, then I would decline the position and spare the church further division. The following is a list of my eleven principles for generating a new vision of a new era.

1. Heritage: We shall maintain our heritage as a Bible Church, i.e., rooted and grounded in the fundamental doctrines of the faith, nondenominational and solid expository teaching of God's Word.

The purpose of this principle is to organize the board around the central aspects of our heritage that we agreed to and all wanted to continue. When you are introducing change, the fear of losing those foundational truths and bedrock values develops inevitably. Some of the most influential members of the congregation felt deeply about this aspect of our heritage. With this being the first statement of commitment, it would give them a greater level of comfort, despite my youth and eagerness to make changes. It should also be noted that, through study of the American religious scene, I believe strongly in nondenominational churches and the practical teaching of the Bible as building blocks for future church growth. These beliefs were not weights to hold us back. This statement, by their absence, also identified what elements of our heritage would not be maintained.

2. Mission-Driven Church: The church must be mission-driven rather than security-driven. We are prepared to take the necessary risks to accomplish the fourfold mandate of Christ to his Church, namely: worship, evangelism, edification, and outreach. Though the mission is fixed, the methods of accomplishing the mission are always subject to change and evaluation. Methodology must not be raised to the level of the sacred so that the church will remain as a relevant witness to its contemporary culture. Our evaluation will be based on how well we accomplish the mission versus how we survive as an organization.

Lyle Schaller states in *Strategies for Change* that a church cannot be focused on the perpetuation of the institution as its central mission if it is to stay innovative and effective for the times.[2] This statement was necessary to hold the leadership accountable when the criticism got rough or the cost got high; we made a pact to take the risk and make the sacrifices necessary when our mission was at stake. It was also my vision that a church could be created and organized intentionally around the fulfillment of its mission. This will be discussed in the next chapter.

3. *Christ as Head:* The church will run with Christ as the Head. The church will be led by the elders as its appointed spiritual leadership. Any acts that seek to subvert this arrangement will not be tolerated.

At first glance, this seems like a harsh and divisive statement, but the elders had lost so much respect from the congregation during the four-year search for a senior minister that they were ineffective. Restoring the elders to leadership was a vital step toward rebuilding the backbone of PBC. Once they were empowered to demonstrate their maturity and authority again, the congregation would respect and honor their strength of leadership. I also wanted the elders to claim responsibility for the decisions we were going to make. I wanted to know who my boss was and minimize the impact of potential power centers that might develop.

4. *Large Church Profile:* PBC will accept its role as a large church in a heavily populated city. It will seek to capitalize on its size and vast resources as a strategic opportunity to provide a full-service program to our segmented and pluralistic society (some of this pluralism is the consequence of the breakdown of the traditional American family unit).

Even with our decline over the last four years, we were still a large church with a great deal to offer. The church leaders needed to think like a large church, not a small church. If we thought large, we could expand and get larger. If we thought small, we would shrink to fit the vision of smallness.

5. *Full-Service Program:* PBC will seek to implement a full-service program of ministries to all groups in the church (senior adults, youth, singles, children), with a primary emphasis upon the largest growing segment of Arlington's population—those forty-five and younger. It will thus be essential for those forty-five and older to have a significant ministry to the future generations of the church of Jesus Christ. Titus 2 highlights this focus as a biblical pattern for the church—for example, the older building into the lives of the younger.

Several goals are emphasized here. First, in order for our church to be effective in the contemporary culture, we had to move beyond a Sunday focus and become a seven-day-a-week church. Second, our community was filled with baby boomers. The demographics provided by the Arlington Chamber of Commerce showed that 40 percent of the people, including children, were between the ages of twenty-five and forty-five. As a thirty-year-old senior minister, I would naturally be most effective reaching those people five years on either side of my age. Finally, this principle posed an ongoing challenge and opportunity to the older members of the congregation that they had an essential role of leadership and modeling for our younger members.

6. Children and Youth: The children and youth shall be an area of intense concentration for PBC. These ministries function as key avenues for outreach into the community.

With a high-quality Christian school (Pantego Christian Academy) and a highly acclaimed summer day camp program, I knew we already had a good foundation to reach the children. Affirming the ministries to the children and youth is a unifying mission of most churches.

7. Lay Leadership and Ministry: The role of the laity will be elevated to an equivalent level as that of the clergy (same value/different function). A strong emphasis will be placed on the revival of lay ministry. We will support the laity in their vision/calling versus coercing them to only fill slots in our programs. One of the goals of the elders and staff is to provide a broad-based vision that acts as a canopy for lay vision.

For the ministry to grow, we would need to transform our Sunday morning crowd into an army of soldiers for Christ. But the military draft is not the way to mobilize a group of people in twenty-first century churches. With church members not as committed to the institution of church as previous generations, we could not simply ask them to fill programs that they sensed were not meeting people's real needs. This acknowledgment helps to disassemble programs that are no longer working.

This principle also outlined the contributions that we, as a growing staff, would make and not make. At one of our leadership rallies, I agreed to "administer" the work of the church if they would be the "ministers." This administrative role would include equipping and training them to do the "work of the ministry" (Eph. 4:11-12). This principle has protected me from burnout these last five years. I consistently get eight hours of sleep a night, exercise daily, have Friday and Saturday off and am home five nights out of seven on an average. This strategy and philosophy enables the senior minister to work smarter, not harder.

8. *Sunday Morning:* Sunday morning will consist of a worship service for believers that also attracts the unchurched (the worship service is a key entry point for the unchurched because it is the culturally accepted activity). The music should be authentic and relevant to a contemporary culture. The message must be biblically based, textually accurate, and maintain a heavy emphasis on application of the text to people's lives. It must be evident that the message is passionate, relevant, and comes to life through the messenger.

In order to reach people in our community, we had to put in place a fast-paced, contemporary service. This would be the most difficult change, and it was important to state this intent up front. With the window of change opened in the critical first year, this would be the best time to implement this change. Without a music director on staff, we did not have the resources to pull off both a traditional and a contemporary music program with quality. With everything pointing to a logical focus on growth in the young family area, the clear choice was to have a service based on contemporary music. This has proved to be a critical decision to the nature and pace of our growth based upon the positive responses of the new people who have entered and stayed in our church over the last five years. Of course, a vocal minority have strongly disagreed with the decisions and have created intense environments at times. However, because the leadership was in agreement from day one, we have not been deterred in our mission.

9. Outreach: We will be committed to a philosophy of outreach that achieves the proper balance between local compassion ministries and global mission endeavors (Acts 1:8).

PBC became well known as an innovative church in the area of missions. We knew it would play a part in our future, but some changes needed to be made. The church's impact in missions was previously reduced to a mere check-writing function. Without real ownership and involvement, I knew that this arm of our work would decline. In addition, because of our focus on the younger generation, hands-on involvement in local social problems was crucial. We would have to do more than write a check; we would have to get our fingernails dirty. Up to this point, active involvement in missions, either local or global, was not the mark of the Bible churches. This part of our heritage had to be overcome. We simply laid out a biblical principle that includes the local ministry. I did not elaborate on the missions statement, because it was not a top priority in my first few years. A church does not grow *because* of cross-cultural ministries, but a growing church can effectively *make a difference* in cross-cultural ministries. The church needed to focus on its own health and growth if the missions program was to be strong. In my fourth year of leadership, we changed the missions paradigm. Those changes are now being implemented. See chapter 10 for more details.

10. PBC as a Model: We will become a model for church leadership for the future through our commitment to Dallas

Theological Seminary. PBC's success will be the catalyst that revitalizes the ailing Bible Church movement (and others open to learning from independent churches) and propels it into the twenty-first century, while maintaining our essential values and forging a new vision for the future.

One thing I notice in my study of successful churches is that the congregations seem to rise to meet the positive stories that their senior pastors tell about them. PBC wanted to survive, and I wanted them to see how we could turn our "lemon into lemonade." We needed to focus on impact, not survival. Not only could we rebuild PBC, but we could also become a real help to other churches in crisis. This statement would build the self-esteem of our body.

The Bible Church movement is nondenominational, but Dallas Theological Seminary is its mother school. When I became the senior minister of PBC, there were five other large Bible churches in the area that were leaderless. Because of our location in the Dallas/Fort Worth metroplex, and because one of the most influential members of our body was a Dallas Seminary professor, we had a real opportunity for growth. This impact has already started to take place through a number of seminars we have conducted at the seminary. I have taken a role in the Center for Christian Leadership to assist pastors around the country in their work through cassette tapes, books, conferences, and other materials. The church is currently pursuing a partnership with the Teaching Church Network to begin helping other churches in decline in a more formal capacity. The most exciting element of this vision has been a pilot program for "church-based seminary training," which we began in January of 1995 in conjunction with Dallas Seminary. The professor mentioned above, who attends our church and is on our staff part-time, received permission to take a one-year sabbatical to assist us in this project.

11. People-Centered Church: PBC must be a people-centered church rather than a program-centered church. Programs should be tools used to maximize ministry to people. People must never be manipulated to maintain the existence of programs. Programs are a means to an end. People are the end.

We knew that several of the current programs had to be eliminated. These programs were draining valuable resources needed elsewhere, yet they had become "sacred cows." It would not be popular to eliminate these programs, but it had to be done. This philosophical statement took the church back to the core reasons of why we have programs. Because programs do not last as long today as they once did, we have the opportunity to turn these "sacred cows" into "hamburger meat." We tell our staff, with tongue in cheek, that it is a lot more fun killing the previous senior minister's programs. If adhered to, this philosophy keeps a church from becoming irrelevant to the needs of its culture.

The initial document that outlined these eleven principles has been replaced by updated revisions, but it served its purpose well. We continue to use the above principles extensively in our development as a church.

CHAPTER V

THE MISSION
From Believer to Disciple

COMEBACK CONCEPTS
1. The change agent must craft a memorable statement that captures the biblical mission for the church that promises to change lives.
2. The mission statement must be used to guide the leadership in its direction and programs. Changes that are made are explained in light of the mission statement.
3. Clearly defined venues must be identified to communicate the mission to the church body repeatedly. A visitor should be able to walk up to any member and receive the mission statement of the church.
4. A vehicle should be established that helps members evaluate their individual spiritual development against the mission statement.

Few organizations care to admit how unused and ineffective their mission statement is. We believe the problem is twofold. First, most mission statements are too broad and unmeasurable. Second and more important, most churches never developed their infrastructures to achieve their mission. So we developed a measurable mission statement in my first year along with the commitment to put a practical infrastructure in place to achieve it.

A Biblical Statement that Promises Life Change

Three principles came into play as our leadership sought to develop a mission statement. First, we knew it had to be biblically based. "What is the mission of the church as found in the pages of the Bible?" Peter Drucker, in a speech given to pastors of large churches, stated that the decline of the liberal churches in America in the early 1900s came as a result of their losing sight of the mission of the church given to them by Christ. "The mission of the church has something to do with Christ's statement that 'He came to seek and to save those who were lost'," Drucker stated.[1] Because of our stated commitment to the Bible, we were set on developing a mission statement that would represent the biblical commission.

A second critical element we wanted our mission statement to represent was the potential changes in lives that result from the Christianity experienced through fellowship with our church. A great deal of evidence proves that present-day people come to church for different reasons than in previous generations. People are looking for a church that is focused on their own life development rather than on a primary commitment to the denomination or institution. Therefore, we wanted a statement that would focus on what people *become* versus what our church *does*.

Finally, we wanted the mission statement to pass the "T-shirt test." Our administrator was at a meeting with Peter Drucker, who was asked by one of the participants about the appropriate length of a mission statement. He responded, "If you can get the mission statement on a T-shirt, then it's probably the appropriate length." We wanted our mission statement to pass this critical test of brevity. In 1993 we actually put it on a T-shirt.

Our mission is to transform people, through the work of the Holy Spirit, into fully developing followers of Christ.

The words, "fully developing followers of Christ," comprise the catch phrase that everyone has picked up and used. For example, while writing this section, we received a letter from one of our people who is on a special missions project to Russia. She writes about her experience: "My study on becoming a fully developed follower of Christ is continuing here." It is exciting as a pastor to see people using this phrase to describe their central goal in life. By no means do we see this statement as unique to our church. Other churches have similar statements. When we developed the statement, we knew it sounded familiar, but we couldn't place it. Months later, we uncovered a popular church that had a statement that is almost identical. However, we feel that this statement is a simple and accurate description of what we are trying to achieve. The real leadership and creativity comes when you try to put the mission statement to work in the lives of people.

Being Mission-Driven—Getting the Mission Into Play

Having the right mission statement is easy compared to the more difficult task of applying it. Peter Drucker describes the "bottom line" for the nonprofit organization. "Board and staff work together to define a clear mission with specific and measurable goals and objectives. Mission guides decision-making by board and staff, and results matter."[2] To help us in this task, we developed a simple profile of what a fully developing follower of Christ looks like. This breakdown of our goal would give us a way to implement our programs and measure our success against the mission statement.

Going back to Acts 2:42-47, we defined four stages toward becoming a fully developed follower of Christ. As a baseball player must touch all four bases to make a home run, so the Christian must run bases in the effort to achieve spiritual maturity. These bases are:

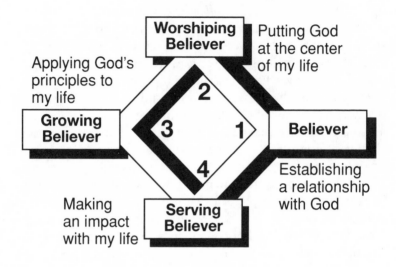

The focus again is on what a person becomes rather than what the organization does. This fourfold description also adds purpose to our programs. It is used as the basis for the elimination or addition of programs based on our body's needs. Whenever a person gets involved in a program of the church, they are conscious of how it directly contributes to their personal spiritual development. We are encouraged to see our congregation embracing this concept, applying it to their lives, and even using our mission terminology, as one member writes:

> Pantego was the end and the beginning. I knew I had always loved God and I later found out that I had been on first base most of my life. It was time to move to second. The batters in my life keep sending out those pop flies and I have to scurry back but, the right pitch is on its way! I can feel it!
>
> My family has begun a wonderful awakening process. (They are still in the dugout and hitting pop flies!) Slowly, their frustrations of having to go to Church on Sundays have disap-

peared because God wants them there, PERIOD. Then, the excuses that "We get a break when Mom is out of town or has Reserve Training," have disappeared because Dad now wants to go. (OOO - that's a concept!) "Why?" you ask. The main reason is you! We appreciate your honesty in being human. We look forward to your wonderful family "trials and tribulations" simply because we experience the same things. You have a way of putting the things we all struggle with into perspective. Your humor, conviction, and acceptance of yourself helps us feel we are not alone and if you can do it, so can we. (Rick [her husband] was sure that I was the only wife that left rooms without turning lights off!!) But, hearing you talk about relationships and pettiness gives us such a great topic for discussion these upcoming weeks. Isn't that what it's all about? This, and so many other examples reinforce the basic fact that we are only human and we must never stop trying to be more Godly. And, while we try, let's laugh.

The Spiritual Fitness Plan

We took the mission statement a step further by designing our assimilation process around it. From the moment a person comes into contact with us, we want to provide assistance in his or her development as a follower of Christ. We agreed to take on the label of a high-commitment church. Lyle Schaller defines the "High-Commitment Church" as a church where the members understand the expectations of personal spiritual growth.[3] The church develops its programs to reflect that commitment. We felt that many people in our area of the country have tried attending church, but they were not satisfied with what they found. We decided that these people would be attracted to a high-commitment church, as long as the commitment was to their spiritual development and not simply to the perpetuation of the institution. This discipleship-driven vision has really excited our growing leadership team.

Before examining the details behind the Spiritual Fitness Plan, we need to look at the basic framework of our assimilation process. Like other growing churches, we are experiencing dynamic worship time in our weekend services. This attracts a significant number of new people each week (8 percent of each worship service represents first-time attendees). These visitors make a choice either to stay with us or move on, so we focus a great deal of our attention on assisting them in discovering our exciting and clear mission and, more important, how they can benefit from becoming involved with us.

There are four major movements in our "front door" assimilation plan:

> Worship Service
> Newcomers Coffee
> New Members Class
> Community Group

We use a "floor plan" drawing to illustrate this process to our growing leadership team.

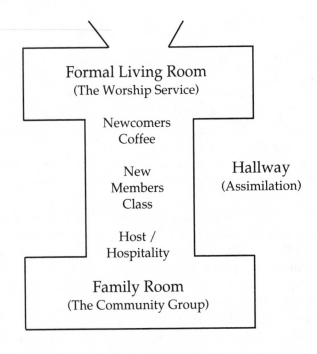

The Worship Service is the Formal Living Room. It is not the place where intimacy takes place; however, it is the place where the host creates an environment that is conducive to guests. The Community Group structure is our Family Room. It is the place where the family of God meets in an informal and intimate setting. Currently we have eighteen such family rooms that consist of approximately fifty people each. These family gatherings meet on Sunday morning, but have a host of other opportunities for family activities. A hallway connects the Formal Living area (the Worship Services) and the Family Room (the Community Group). The hallway defines the core of our assimilation strategy. The primary vehicles used to implement this strategy are the Newcomers Coffee and the New Members Class.

A person comes into one of our worship services through the invitation or recommendation from one of our members or regular attendees. The goal of that service, outside of leading the people into meaningful worship, is to move the guest to an informal yet informative reception, currently held once a month on Sunday evenings. It is at this reception or Newcomers Coffee that people are introduced to the mission of the church and are encouraged to take the third step—attending the New Members Class. People are given the opportunity at the Coffee to sign up for the Membership Class. It is through this class, taught on two consecutive Wednesday evenings, that new people begin to significantly engage in the mission of the church.

To develop this assimilation process through the membership class, we looked for a metaphor that the people would readily understand and relate to our mission. It didn't take long until we settled on a fitness metaphor. We felt that this metaphor would work because the Bible draws on it to address the subject of spiritual development. Here are a few examples from Paul's writings:

God wants you to be a winner!

Do you not know that in a race the runners run, but only one gets the prize? Run in such a way as to get the prize. (1 Cor. 9:24)

Winning takes training and development.

Have nothing to do with godless myths and old wives' tales; train yourself to be godly. For physical training is of some value, but godliness has value for all things, holding promise for both the present life and the life to come. (1 Tim. 4:7-8)

Everyone who competes in the games goes into strict training. They do it to get a crown of laurel that will not last; but we do it to get a crown that will last forever. Therefore, I do not run like a man running aimlessly; I do not fight like a man shadow boxing. No, I beat my body and make it my slave so that after I have preached to others, I myself will not be disqualified for the prize. (1 Cor. 9:25-27)

Play by the rules.

Similarly, if anyone competes as an athlete, he does not receive the victor's crown unless he competes according to the rules. (2 Tim. 2:5)

Our culture is also enamored with physical fitness. The fitness craze has gone far beyond a mere fad and has proven to be an integral part of our society for some time. The use of this metaphor would not only yield heightened understanding but also attraction. We needed to convey that it is just as attractive to be spiritually fit as it is to be physically fit.

We looked at the strategy of the health and fitness clubs. I understood this as well as anyone. After having back surgery in the earlier part of 1992, I needed to design a personal fitness program that would help me develop physically. At my health club, a physical fitness consultant asked me for a brief history of my health as well as my personal fitness goals. I told him of my back surgery as well as three specific personal goals. The consultant then took out a fitness planner and proceeded to lay out an easy and targeted plan for my development. There were 250 or more different things to do in this club, but I only needed to focus on ten. I work out alongside people who are pure fitness "hunks" as well as some who are even further behind than me. The key is that though we are all at different levels of fitness, we are working out a plan that defines where we are, not where we once were or simply wish we were.

"What if we could do this as a church?" I thought. The staff loved the idea and we went to work. After multiple brainstorming and planning meetings with the management staff, we developed a plan with three central features to it—the Spiritual Fitness Planner, a Spiritual Fitness Resource Card, and a Spiritual Fitness Coach.

The Spiritual Fitness Planner is equivalent to the fitness planner one fills out at the health club. It looks at a person's history, goals, and action plan. The person begins the process by taking stock of his or her spiritual history. Personal evaluation is made on a scale of 1 to 6 in twelve key areas. These areas represent a further definition of a worshiping, growing, and serving believer. The planner has a place for three personal spiritual goals to be established as well as three family goals (if applicable). Finally, the planner calls for the goals to be developed into a specific, measurable, and achievable action plan. (See Appendix A.)

The Spiritual Fitness Resource Card (see Appendix B) provides a list of all the resources that the church offers to help a person develop in the areas evaluated. These include a biblical literacy class for those who feel they do not understand the basics of the Bible; a full physical fitness program such as aerobics, self-defense, and exercise classes for new moms who get back into shape by doing exercises with their infants (Moms with Tots); a seminar that helps parents discover their child's unique design; Integrity Groups for men who want assistance in making the right or best decisions for their marriages, family, work, personal life, and so on; a "Master Your Money" class for those who evaluated their financial stewardship as a weak area in their spiritual life. A follow-up class is offered for those who want to go into our computer lab, which is set up for our private school, and be coached in the use of a popular money management software program.

We also felt it was important to list resources outside of the church. This is a practice that demonstrates our integrity to serve a person's spiritual needs over the concerns of the institution. We provide a listing of Christian radio stations, free Christian publications, high-quality family conferences, counseling services, and more.

Finally, there is **the Spiritual Fitness Coach.** The coach is the one who personalizes the process described above. He or she is trained and given the mission of working with four new people a month. They work these four people through the complete process by using the planner and resource card. The coach completes his or her obligation by following up one month later by phone to see how the person is doing in getting the chosen goals in action. This is also a process that feeds back to the leadership on how well the various ministries of our church are doing in getting new people involved. For example, if a new person sets out a plan to enhance his or her personal devotion and worship by signing up for our "Experiencing God" class, then we want to ensure that the leadership of that ministry is doing their job in receiving this new person. The coach gives us a report card on our assimilation process in that first critical month after a person decides to become involved with us.

We strongly believe that this process cannot stop within the first year. It would only make sense that the person who is here the longest would model the process of setting spiritual goals. So the process is continued in our small group ministry, which will be described later. Every year during the months of November and December, all of our small groups go through a reevaluation of their spiritual lives and set new goals in the context of a safe and supportive group of ten people they have come to love.

Communicating the Mission

We have already shared how the new person hears and engages in the mission of PBC. But it can't stop there; it must go deeper. Our leadership team has developed other strategies and vehicles to communicate our mission. Here are five:

1. The mission statement of the church is printed on every church document, brochure, and bulletin.
2. The mission of the church is stated clearly at least one time in every worship service.
3. T-shirts with our logo on the front and this inscription on the back—"I'm a fully developing follower of Christ"—are made readily available.
4. A monthly leadership rally is held, where the mission statement is recited by everyone.
5. The mission statement is put on a "business card" and passed out at most functions.

Getting the mission into play didn't begin my first day on the job. It has taken every ounce of available time to make the creations and improvements that we have currently in place. All the people becoming members know the mission and even claim it as their own personal goal. However, some of the people who have been at the church for more than three years feel lost and disconnected. To remedy the problem, we have embarked on a practical strategy.

We have taken the New Members Class material on our mission and spiritual fitness and turned it into an eight-week Sunday series with the purpose of introducing it to those who have been in our church for more than three years. Here is a listing of the eight weeks we covered:

Week 1: God Wants You to Be a Winner
Week 2: The Four Bases of Spiritual Development
Week 3: 1st Base: Establishing a Relationship with God
Week 4: Principles of Spiritual Development, Part 1
Week 5: Principles of Spiritual Development, Part 2
Week 6: 2nd Base: Putting God at the Center of My Life
Week 7: 3rd Base: Applying God's Principles to My Life
Week 8: Home Plate: Making an Impact with My Life

Looking back over these first few years of establishing new wineskins for a traditional and dying church, we realize that having a clearly defined mission not only gave the church a boost but also gave me the incentive to identify my own personal mission in light of the big picture.

CHAPTER VI

A NEW ROLE
FOR THE GOVERNING BOARD

COMEBACK CONCEPTS

1. The governing board must have real spiritual authority to make decisions regarding the direction and changes necessary to revitalize and revision the declining church.
2. The senior minister cannot move ahead of the governing board.
3. There must be a solid bond of trust between the senior minister and the board for the revitalization process to even have a chance of working.
4. The governing board must stand behind the senior minister 100 percent as he implements necessary changes. Necessary confrontation must take place within the boardroom, not in front of the congregation.
5. A simple process must be created that enables the governing board to interface with the congregation without having to micro-manage the senior minister and staff.

Without a doubt, a unified board of leaders is essential to leading a church through a rough transition of change. I banked on my relationship and unity with the governing board to get the church back on its feet again. It is in this area that I have made some wise and unwise decisions. One of my staff members once said, "You can make many small mistakes and still be effective; you cannot make the big ones." Anything shy of a strong relationship with your board is a big mistake. Howard Hendricks, a professor at Dallas Theological Seminary, wisely warned me that a poor relationship between the senior pastor and the governing board is the major reason for unnecessary and divisive conflict in thousands of congregations. Even though I have made some small mistakes in this area, I still enjoy a wonderful relationship and common bond of trust and respect with my board.

The Cardinal Rule of Church Comebacks: Don't Move Ahead of Your Governing Board

It was understood that we could withstand a great deal of pressure during our period of change if our board was unified. Constitutionally, our governing board is made up of seven to nine members, with the senior pastor serving as an additional member. One-third of the board rotates off every year. The terms are for three years. A board member can serve two consecutive three-year terms, after which the person must take at least one year off.

The selection of these three new members each year is critical to the continuity of our mission. New members to the board are selected by the existing elders and three at-large members of the congregation. We made an agreement that the candidates would not simply be those who had been at the church for many years but those who embraced the mission and were engaged positively in contributing to that mission. This has worked beautifully. While it is extremely healthy to have open dialogue and even disagreement within the scope of the vision, it is unproductive to constantly challenge the basic direction.

Two basic commitments are made to each other as board and pastor.

1. The board will not micro-manage me. They would not try to run the operations of this complex organization but

would, instead, allow me to organize a staff team to get the job done.

For example, I pick my staff. On every occasion I have received their counsel, but it is my decision. If I am going to be responsible for the staff and the results, I should be able to select them. If the staff team is not working, then I would rather be replaced than work under the complexity of a board-led staff.

2. I will not move ahead of the board. My goal is to keep them informed. No surprises. The board works with me on setting vision and policy. They then oversee my implementation of that vision based on results. Once a decision is made, it is my responsibility to develop plans and implement the policy, program, or process. I must not implement major policy that has not been established with the elders. I must keep the elders informed of the progress. We have a saying among the staff, "If you are one step ahead of the people, you're a leader; if you're ten steps ahead of them, you're a martyr."

Time Together Builds Trust

Central to these operating values is trust. I must trust the board and they must trust me. For the board to make its decisions under this scenario, we established that only once-a-month meetings were necessary. However, a problem emerges with this strategy. The board can easily become detached from the heart of the work even though their minds are involved. In my second year, I concentrated on executing our plans. The board maintained their end of the deal by giving me the authority to go after it. At the same time, I began to notice a slight detachment from the work. It went on for some time during that second year before I realized that though the elders knew the church was recovering, they felt left out of the process. They felt decreasing ownership. I knew I needed to revise the strategy with the elders to give them a real part in the ownership of the work without violating the "micro-managing rule."

The board went on a retreat to discuss this issue. The following text represents what we decided to do about our problem.

Simple Structure for Maximum Impact

We started by identifying the major groups in our body, which we placed in four circles concentrically. For the elders to keep the heart for the ministry, they needed to touch each one of those circles without having to manage any of them.

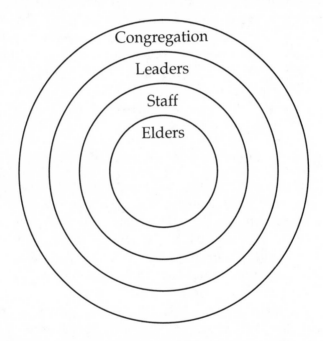

Elders: The elders decided to meet weekly to maintain a deep fellowship with one another. This has turned out to be one of the best small groups in our church. We chose Monday nights to accommodate business people in our group who travel. The board members make it a priority to lay over, whenever possible, on Monday and begin their travel on Tuesday.

Staff: We wanted the staff and board to know one another. We have developed a management team of three staff members who oversee everything that goes on in our church. (By the way, as the senior pastor, I do not oversee any programs in the church. I get involved in many aspects of the church, but I am not responsible for direct management of any of them. This frees me up to stay focused on the "big picture.") These three members attend the weekly meeting and have developed a great relationship with our board. I only have one cardinal rule for these three staff members: "You cannot introduce any new ideas or thoughts in the boardroom that have not been previously discussed as a staff management team." I think it is important for the staff to enter the boardroom as a unified team. We can openly discuss new ideas and differences in our weekly staff meetings.

Leadership: We have several hundred people who make up the leadership or serving segment of our body. We gather these people together on the first Sunday afternoon of the month for a two-hour leadership rally. The elders are present at this meeting to mingle with the various leadership teams. They are called upon to pray and to officially "commission" our new leaders into ministry. Because they have all committed to being at this important meeting, they do not meet on the corresponding first Monday night of each month.

Congregation: With a congregation our size and growing, it is impossible for a band of nine people to even begin to touch the extent of hurts and needs. We have created our Community Group structures to realistically handle the shepherding and nurturing needs of our people. However, we want the elders to stay in touch with them. I have devised two very simple systems for achieving this goal.

1. As pointed out earlier, our board meets on Monday nights. These meetings begin at 7:00 P.M. and last until 10:00 P.M. In the first hour, our board members pray. Each Sunday we get a

list of prayer requests from members of the congregation. Each request is prayed for by name.

I write these requests down and give them to my office assistant on Tuesday morning. She takes the list and creates a postcard-size note, which is mailed to every person named in prayer for the previous night. Here is a sample of a card sent out:

Dear John,

On October 18, the Elders of Pantego Bible Church prayed that your surgery on Tuesday would go well. We asked God to heal your knee and restore you to full mobility.

We wanted you to know that we care and are thinking about you. We also believe in the power of prayer and know that God is at work on your behalf. Hold onto your faith!

In Christ,

Ed Frazier
Elder Board Chairman

The elders have received numerous calls, letters, and unexpected visits during services from people who were deeply moved when they received their note from the board. Some still carry their card in their purses and wallets to this day. One man, who was in the process of having his business closed down, says that he taped the card on his bathroom mirror to encourage him every morning before he went back into the "trenches."

2. The second practical and simple strategy we implemented was a visitation program. From 7:00 P.M. to 9:00 P.M. every

Monday night, two of our board members, on a rotation basis, go out and visit members. These visits are arranged by my office on Monday morning. While the rest of the group is praying in our conference room, two are actually out visiting. When they return at 9:00 P.M., they give a report of their visits. This simple process enables the board to touch 150 to 200 families in our church in a given year. While it does not begin to make a dent in meeting all the congregation's needs, it does give our elders a real sense of the heart of the ministry. They love it!

To this very day, I have a great and deep relationship of trust with the elders of the church. If this ever breaks down beyond repair, my days of effectiveness are numbered. I pray that God gives me the wisdom to not let this happen.

CHAPTER VII

THE DEVELOPMENT OF THE STAFF TEAM

> ### COMEBACK CONCEPTS
> 1. Building your own team takes about five years.
> 2. There is no sense in starting something new unless you have factored in the resources and staffing necessary to sustain it.
> 3. During the revitalization process look at fulfilling many of your staffing needs from within the church with part-time positions.
> 4. Position your staff according to their gifts and manage them

I am absolutely sure that when it comes to making a comeback in an established church, YOU CAN'T DO IT ALONE! Whether you are a small church, a medium-sized church, or a large church, you must have a team around you to execute the mission. Even if you had the time to do everything, you are not gifted to do everything. Many pastors get into trouble by agreeing to be like someone else.

It is important to note that a strong board must precede a strong staff in importance. Why? The staff is called upon to implement change but it is the board who must first approve the change and then wholeheartedly support it. A staff cannot survive the revisioning process if a strong board is not in place.

Not every church is large enough to have a paid staff. But every church that seeks to improve its ministry must have a team of highly committed people around the leader if the mission is to be executed. A large church does not eliminate the need for a large volunteer army of leaders. It simply has become large enough to require a layer of management and support necessary to run efficiently and effectively. Pantego Bible Church currently has twenty lay shepherds over groups of fifty people with each one having an apprentice in training. That is just within our adult ministries. If I was in a small church, I would build a team of volunteers and call them staff. A change agent is typically focused on orchestrating the next step in the plan for a comeback and thinking about the next five steps. Once a positive change has been instituted, it must be sustained. As a matter of fact, the change agent should not even institute a major change unless he has factored in the necessary resources to staff the maintenance of that change.

Principles of Staffing

I laid out some general principles of staffing at the beginning of my work that have served me well.

1. I will staff to directly help us achieve our mission.

Many churches possess a progressive mission statement and discuss many "cutting edge" ideas, but build their staff around the traditional paradigm with standard job descriptions. If helping people become serving believers by identifying their spiritual gifts is a critical part of your vision, then it must also be a key component of a staff or lay leader's role. That staff or lay leader's work is evaluated on how many people discovered their gifts in a given month and whether or not they identified the process as a meaningful spiritual experience. (See page 85 for a description of how we have currently structured our staff to achieve our mission.)

2. I will staff according to my overall implementation plan.

I did not concentrate on everything at once. The area I concentrated on was typically the area I staffed at that time. Things that were dead, I left buried. Things that were broken and not as essential as something else, I killed or ignored. We have developed a fond affection for the adage, "When the horse is dead, dismount."

3. I will staff in my area of weakness.

I knew that the vast majority of my time would flow toward my weaknesses. I identified those areas where I was deficient and not particularly motivated and staffed them first. I put a high premium on enjoying life. This led me to hire a business administrator in my first year. All the systems needed to be rebuilt. Because we have a large private school, our property maintenance and scheduling are very complex. After doing the job for six months, I knew it was a major distraction for me. I hired an administrator so I could be more effective in my areas of responsibility.

4. I will hire part-time staff whenever possible.

One of the reasons for this is the astronomical rise in the cost of fringe benefits. If you hire part-time staff you are not bound to provide many of these costly benefits. Second, when you are taking on a comeback project, you can be assured that the resources needed are far greater than the funds available. You have to develop a creative stair-step approach to get your ideas into play. Third, we are sandwiched between two large seminaries. We have access to a great resource of people who are itching to get their hands in the ministry while they are still in training. Next, there are a number of women in our church whose schedules made it ideal for them to work a part-time job. As an area of ministry grew and developed, I either moved part-timers to a full-time position, or I hired a team of part-time people to handle the job. I experienced exceptional success with both strategies.

5. I will look for much of my staff from within the church.

While I'm not against hiring from the outside, I have found that due to the cost and unknowns, hiring a person from the outside often does not work. A person on the inside knows and understands the mission, knows the culture, and believes in our purpose. It can take up to a year or more for an outsider to acquire a working knowledge of these same areas. On top of that, you never know what you are really getting into with an outside person. The résumé and references are always slighted. You have a mess when you move a person to your city only to discover that it is not a match. I am also discovering that our church has become a great place to train future church leaders; many of the existing churches are simply not dealing with the innovative ministries necessary to carry them into the twenty-first century. I risk making a mistake by hiring an individual from the other side of the country who is experiencing ministry in a dated paradigm. Outside of four people, two of whom were for the same part-time position, I have hired all my staff internally.

6. I will look for staff who have demonstrated Christian character, commitment, and competence in ministry.

Seminary degrees and denominational ordinations are becoming less and less important to innovative churches. More important is a verification of character, personal commitment to the work, and ministry competence for the specific job assignment in question. When it comes to our staffing positions we have decided that we want someone who has a history of success in doing the job. If not, the job either does not get done, or you have to do it yourself. In a growing church neither is an option. The only workable alternative is to hire someone for the job who can do it. However, simply having a person who can perform a job but does so in a manner that devalues people, runs over people, or lacks integrity, is not only wrong but also creates volumes of painstaking work to undo the damage. When a staff member leads and manages from principle, his or her work empowers others to build the work in the most effective way possible.

7. I will look not only at a person's gifts and experience but also at the way they will affect the overall team.

In one situation, I had found a highly competent person to fill a very important role on our team. In the end, I decided not to hire him on the simple basis that his temperament was too similar to two of my other key players. I felt this would cause a great imbalance to our team.

Two Bedrock Values

I have two key values that have guided me through some rough decisions. When you are revitalizing a congregation, it means that you are restructuring it. If it grows, it requires further restructuring. Everyone on the staff must continue to develop and discover how they are going to fit into the next restructuring. These two values have enabled us to get through the five or so restructurings that have taken place in the last five years.

1. Everyone will be placed in a position of responsibility that fits the individual's makeup as a person.

One of the most unjust things a church can do is to position a good person in the wrong place. To facilitate this, we do a battery of assessments on each staff member before that person is hired. The DOMA Group, under the leadership of Ralph Mattson, has assisted us from day one. I outlined a basic understanding of the assessment on page 44. We now have a trained person on staff to help our team understand their God-given uniqueness and talent.

2. If I have to make a change in staff, I will do so in a win/win fashion.

As a church grows, it often requires different people to meet its changing needs. If a staff member is experiencing some difficulty, we will aggressively undertake the positioning of people beside that person who can shore up their weaknesses. This often involves hiring just the right support staff. If this still does not remedy the situation, I will try to reposition that person. If that still does not work out, dismissal is the last alternative. At this point, I believe it is the most dignified and right thing to do to honor a brother or sister in Christ. I will assist them in finding a new job.

Managing for Results

When you assemble a winning team, the only way to manage them is on results. This makes my job easier and gives the staff a real sense of authority with their corresponding responsibilities. Every staff member has about five distinct questions that he or she must answer for his or her area each month, based on the tracking of results. For example, the adult pastor is asked, "How many people are in small groups this month compared to last month, last year, and our goals?" Another question: "How many apprentices are identified in the small groups for future leadership this month compared to last month, last year and our goals?" My administrator takes the information submitted and puts it into an overall report of graphs and charts that compares the results with last month, last year, and the targeted goal. This gives me an opportunity to spot problems and trends on a monthly basis before things get out of hand. If you do not have a staff that you can manage by an emphasis on results, you probably do not have a staff that can grow with the church.

As our church has grown, so has our team. Recently, I met with my staff to introduce the development of the next structure. **We are attempting to put into place the concept of**

Self-Directed Work Teams. I have selected three full-time staff members to serve **as team leaders for three critical teams.**

Team #1: The Worshiping Believer/Win
Focus: Moving people from the community into membership
Team #2: The Growing Believer/Build
Focus: Moving people from membership into biblical community and discipleship
Team #3: The Serving Believer/Send
Focus: Moving people from biblical community into leadership
(See Appendix C for staff organization chart according to the Self-Directed Work Team concept.)

The first five years have involved change. The next five will involve implementing and managing those changes. I must turn over this phase of our work to the team while I look to new horizons for our church. At the end of the second five years, the church will need to face another stretching challenge. Instead of recovering from a crisis, it needs to be a planned challenge of outreach.

Another goal I have is to provide the spiritual leadership for our large team. I believe that this will be easier when I am not directly responsible for so many details. The staff is excited about the opportunity to take on the next challenge.

CHAPTER VIII

PREPARING
FOR THE TWENTY-FIRST CENTURY

COMEBACK CONCEPTS

1. Significant changes take an average of two years to fully implement. As the church moves out of the crisis, the window for change slightly closes, requiring more time to implement major change.
2. The church of the twenty-first century must have a well-defined, step-by-step, intentional process of how it will achieve its mission in the lives of people.
3. Revitalizing a declining congregation almost always involves revisioning the Sunday morning service. The church service of the twenty-first century must not compromise the truth of the message but must put more creative energy into getting the message across.
4. The church of the twenty-first century must be good at establishing authentic biblical community where people can grow together.
5. The church of the twenty-first century must learn how to effectively place and manage volunteers.
6. The goal of the revitalization process is not to increase the number of programs but to get really good at a few critical ones.

As the months rolled by and as new people came to our church, we realized what had brought us to this point would not carry us into the twenty-first century. We recognized that if we did not continue to make more changes in keeping with the times, our church would fall further behind in the mission of reaching new generations. None of the changes have altered the message of the Bible. They are changes of form, not substance. We did not tackle everything at once, but there were several major changes going at one time. Some of the changes were in the implementation phase while others were just beginning to be discussed. For the most part, each of these changes has taken an average of two years to get on-line.

In many ways, I feel I have had an advantage coming from outside of the church. I had been in churches all my life but wasn't sure how to run one. I came from the world of business and the nonprofit organization. Joel Barker, in his book *Discovering the Future,* says that it often takes a person from outside an industry to see the next horizon.[1] As Marshall McLuhan once said, "We don't know who discovered water, but we can be pretty sure it wasn't a fish." I approached planning on what seemed to make sense rather than on traditions with which I was not familiar.

Intentional Systems

Peter Senge, in his book *The Fifth Discipline,* identifies five key characteristics of tomorrow's organization.[2] The "fifth discipline" is **systems thinking.** The new organizations of today and tomorrow must have clearly defined systems in place to get the job done.

What implications does this have on the church? The church of the twenty-first century must create a step-by-step approach to accomplish its mission in people's lives. Some innovative churches are calling this the "Purpose-Driven Church," while others are calling it "Intentional Discipleship." At PBC, we have outlined very simple and specific systems and steps on how we move people from one level of spiritual growth to another. Our Spiritual Fitness Plan is one example of how we achieve this goal (see chapter 5). Because of the tremendous diversity in our world today, it is critical for people to have systems in place that enable them to customize a plan that meets their unique needs. A "one size fits all" approach will not work in the church of the twenty-first century.

The Sunday Service

The very first major change I made was in the Sunday service. This is where the personality of a church is established, and I wanted the personality of our church to be positive, alive, relevant, and real. The best way to achieve this with the people we would most likely reach was to install a contemporary service. The greatest opportunity to achieve this was in the first few months when people were the most open to change. We knew up front that we would lose people in our first year no matter what we did. This change was made to create a more promising future.

We moved away from the traditional format of the larger choral program to smaller worship groups, which typically accompany a contemporary format. Without a full-time music director and the loss of people over a four-year period, the program in its present state was bordering on embarrassment. Many people were relieved when we introduced a simplified format.

Our next goal was to find a full-time director. We changed the title of this role from Music Director to Worship Pastor to highlight the importance of meaningful worship and downplay the emphasis on music. The people of PBC needed to be rallied around the mission statement. The bottom line of worship puts God, not music, at the center of our lives. It took much longer than we had expected to find the right person to fill this role. He stayed with us for only a year and a half, but did an outstanding job at leading our congregation into worship.

In 1993, we decided to change the worship team's structure. One thing we have learned about worship leaders is that the best of them are artists and performers, not managers. The worship and music was going great, but there were other areas we desired to see come together. We wanted our services to communicate a thematic whole. We wanted to take one simple, biblical, relevant theme and build a service around that theme. We wanted the service to challenge the intellect, emotion, and will of the partaker. We wanted the service to tap into the multiple senses of our people—visual, hearing, touch, and so on.

To accomplish this, we hired a program director who had a marketing background as well as a solid theological education and a manager's temperament. We then hired a new worship leader, who is extremely gifted as a writer, artist, and performer. Together, with a team of gifted volunteers, they execute what has come to be internally known as an "impact service." The goal is life change.

For example, our team put together a creative series called "A Guide to Christian Family Living." We chose ten themes we wanted to communicate. Then we selected popular television shows that would depict these themes. We created the following card to use as both a tool to communicate with our own people and as an invitation our people could use to interest their friends, coworkers, and family members.

We developed each service around the single-sentence theme. For example, as illustrated by the card, on June 6, we did a service called "Father Knows Best." The theme was Family Values. Here is a brief outline of the service and how we developed the theme.

Prelude: Five minutes before the service began, we played Dan Fogelberg's hit, "The Leader of the Band," a song that expresses the musician's beautiful relationship with his father. While this song played, slides were being flashed on a screen to relay some critical announcements as well as to introduce the morning's theme.

A GUIDE To Christian Family Living

April 11 - June 13

Sunday
9:30 A.M.
11:00 A.M.

April **11** **HOME IMPROVEMENT**
Christ Makes the Difference

18 **THE DATING GAME**
Choosing a Mate for a Lifetime

25 **THE NEWLYWED GAME**
Surviving the First Year

May **2** **STEP BY STEP**
The Art of Blended Family Living

9 **THE WONDER YEARS**
Life with Little Kids

16 **PERFECT STRANGERS**
When Your Mate Is Not a Christian

23 **WHEEL OF FORTUNE**
Marriage and Money

30 **LIFE GOES ON**
When Tragedy Strikes

June **6** **FATHER KNOWS BEST**
Family Values

13 **EMPTY NEST**
Life After Kids

Tune in to **Pastor Randy Frazee** as he hosts
this new series, live at **9:30 A.M. & 11:00 A.M.**

Here on PBC *"Your Family Living Channel"*
Pantego Bible Church - Arlington, TX

Songs of Praise and Worship: We sang three contemporary songs and two older hymns that all focused on God, the Father.

Solo: A male member of the vocal group sang a solo entitled "Guard Your Heart," a song challenging fathers to maintain their fidelity and faithfulness to their families.

Thematic Introduction: The program director introduced the theme for the morning by tying all the elements together. He set the scene for the drama that would follow.

Drama: The Pantego Players performed a drama entitled "Family Snapshots, Take II." This drama dealt with a family who was playing a board game that posed situational ethics questions to each other. It brought out how difficult it is to live out the values we think we hold.

Message: I immediately followed the drama. My message dealt with five key family values for today's Christian family.

Response: I introduced a four-by-six-inch "Family Values" card containing five specific ways to apply our theme to the congregation's lives. Each family member was to check areas they felt they would try to apply and turn that card in during the offering. One of the five applications was for first-time visitors. Each Sunday we offer a free cassette of that day's service to every first-time visitor as a gift from the church.

Offering: The offering was taken. People put in their offering for the week and their response card.

Announcement: The people were reminded of the upcoming Father's Day concert. The plans for that day would include everyone arriving at 5:30 P.M. to get their family's picture taken by a group of professional, volunteer photographers in our congregation. The family picture would be developed and put in a cardboard frame that read, "I Love My Dad." As people waited to get their picture taken, the kids would treat dad to ice cream with all the toppings. At 6:30 P.M., everyone made their way into the Worship Center for a concert performed by a popular contemporary Christian artist who has written several family-oriented songs.

Benediction: I read a closing benediction that dismissed the congregation.

Postlude: The worship band played a song entitled "I Choose to Look," another song with a father theme.

People who attend my monthly Newcomers Coffee have testified to the significance of our services in drawing them to the church and causing significant life change in them. I believe I could have started in another, less controversial area, but not with the same dramatic results this change has caused. Without question, it is this area in which I have received the greatest amount of criticism. I think that is true of most churches. The music department is, as Lyle Schaller and many others label it, the "war department of the church."[3] However, the board has stood by me and the positive growth has helped to silence the cynics.

The Relationally Structured Church

Shortly after we tackled the initial changes within the Sunday service, we decided to approach the development of our relational groups. We knew that people were looking for a sense of community and ultimately would stay at a church only if they developed significant relationships.

Of all the structures we looked at, we are the most convinced of the one shared by C. Peter Wagner of the Fuller Institute.[4] He proposes that a healthy church has three, different-sized groups within it. There is the **Celebration** size, which is the largest gathering in the church. In our case, it is the Sunday service with over twelve hundred people in it. This large size is ideal for worship and celebration. Any church with less than four to five hundred in attendance has a difficult time creating this important dynamic. The second group size is **Congrega-**

tion. These are mid-size groups of about fifty people in each. The final group size for a healthy church is the **Cell.** This is a group where intimate relationships are formed.

We preferred this structure and set out to put it in place. Our strategy for the Celebration gathering was working out well. We chose to focus next on the Congregation for several reasons. First, the church already had adult Sunday classes in place. It was positive, as well as practical, to build upon something the church already had in place. Second, there were virtually no other small groups meeting. It would be much harder to start these small groups without first building the mid-size groups at PBC.

We decided to transform the adult Sunday school classes into biblical communities. They would not function simply as education centers, but as churches within a church. They would teach one another, encourage one another and hold one another's hands during a crisis. We wanted these groups to become everything that the Body of Christ was intended to be. Even though the group would still gather on Sunday mornings, it would not be their sole opportunity for interaction. We wanted these people to get involved in one another's lives. Instead of discipling through traditional class structures, we wanted to achieve our developmental mission through a relational structure.

The first step was to change the name to match the purpose, hence the name "Community Groups." The second step was to identify a group of leaders in our congregation who could serve as Community Group Shepherds. These people, mostly couples, would become the pastors over congregations of fifty people. The next step was to write a manual that laid out the function of these groups and their leadership. Here are the key functions of a Community Group.

Biblical Education: An obvious and central mark of a Bible church is the teaching of the Bible. However, most Bible churches have simply become teaching centers where people come to hear the "professional expound the Word." We knew we had a great opportunity to expand the vision of our heritage by devising a personal study program in sync with our teaching as a church. We adopted a model that others were promoting and using with great success, such as Serendipity and Bible Study Fellowship. I outline a series I plan to do on Sunday morning, like a study on the book of Philippians. We then offer a study guide that corresponds to the same material or passage we are covering in the services. The person commits to engaging in personal Bible study by purchasing the study guide and then completing the study during the week. They attend their Community Groups on Sunday morning. These groups sit in a circle and a teacher leads the class in a discussion of the passage. The individual then comes to the service and hears me speak on the same passage. We have been doing this for four years, and it has worked well to communicate and practice a critical part of the mission of our church, i.e., become a growing believer, a fully developing follower of Christ. As a result we have six hundred adults who have committed to the personal study of God's Word. The testimony of life change has greatly encouraged all those who have invested time into this strategy. The following illustrates what some of our people are saying.

> The compartmentalized approach to church has been around for a long time, with the church service and "Sunday School" not having much in common. The simple, but strategic, change to connect the two via a common Bible study has revolutionized my Sunday morning experience. The focal point is now my weekly Bible study. I am more faithful in completing my lesson because I know that both the Community Group discussion and the sermon will be on this common ground. The impact on my retention and application of Scripture has been profound.

The teacher is responsible for teaching and facilitating discussion of the series being studied. Each Saturday morning all the teachers gather to be led in a discussion by a local seminary professor, who also serves part-time on our staff. We found that the shepherd and teacher needed to be two different people for two reasons. One, the gifts of shepherding and mercy are different from the gifts of teaching. What makes one a good teacher doesn't necessarily make that person a good caregiver. Seminaries and churches have learned important lessons, mostly through trial and error, as they have trained aspiring ministers or have hired them. What makes a good teacher doesn't necessarily make for a competent leader. Second, even the most committed volunteer only has so much time to invest. We wanted them to do one thing well versus two things poorly. We wanted them to succeed, and they have.

Caregiving: Transferring the care of our people to these networks of believers was critical to the fulfillment of our mission. A large church that tries to execute this important function through a centralized office is one that has chosen a bottleneck strategy. The board and staff in a large church must equip caregivers and outline their responsibilities, but they cannot be the central vehicle for primary care. They can provide the needed secondary care.

A decentralized system means that the group is executing care without the approval of the central office. The care that is given by a Community Group is tailored to meet the needs of each person in that group. Members of these groups are intelligent and can figure out what needs to be done to minister to its people. For example, the benevolence decisions of the church have been decentralized and given to these leaders. They have rallied, through the use of a simple system, on numerous occasions to meet the financial needs of one in their community. It has been my privilege to catch a small group of people "huddling" together to brainstorm on how to meet the needs of someone in their Community Group.

Small Groups: Instead of creating another structure for our small groups, I decided, along with the staff and other key leaders, to form these groups within our Community Group structure. If a Community Group has fifty people in it, then it can accommodate five small groups of ten. This strategy would allow people to deepen their relationships with a group in which they are already familiar in the larger, Community Group setting.

Each small group formed can select a purpose or type of group that they will become, based on the needs of that group. The primary role of the Community Group shepherd is to develop and nurture the small group leaders.

Community Life: A healthy family plans time for vacations or fun outings. The same is true for a healthy Community Group. Each Community Group has a social coordinator who is responsible for scheduling some sort of group-wide activity six times a year. These events can be picnics, baseball games, camping trips, dinners, and so on.

The training process for Community Group leaders/coordinators is critical. We have several avenues for developing leadership skills in this group.

1. Classroom Instruction: For example, every small group leader has to go through our three-week Small Groups Orientation Class. Though we believe in classroom instruction, we do not feel it is the only place to train leaders any more than we believe that seminaries are the only places to train pastors.

2. Apprenticeships: Every leader in a Community Group is required to select an apprentice. This person walks alongside the leader for the purpose of one day filling that job.

3. Leadership Community: Once a month, we get all of our leaders together in a room. I expound on the vision of the church and tell stories of success we experienced in the last month. Each Community Group leadership team then spends an hour and a half "huddling." It is here that they report, troubleshoot, plan, and pray as a team. Following this "huddle" time, we will often bring the group back together for training in the skills necessary for effective ministry.

All of our Community Groups are formed around a common life experience (e.g., single, young married, parents with teens, single parents, senior citizens, empty nesters, and so on). As a Community Group approaches fifty attendees, we begin to discuss the plans to "launch" or start another Community Group. One of the decisions we made is to "district" our Community Groups. We are starting to see a larger group of people come from a broader driving distance. We are seeing a trend from being a neighborhood church to a metroplex church. We felt that it would be important for new groups to form around defined geographical areas to enhance the sense of real community. While we do not force this structure on new people coming in, we find it to be very attractive to them.

We have gone from four floundering adult Sunday school classes to twenty-five vibrant Community Groups with several new ones always in the making. While there is still improvement needed in effectively delegating the ministry to the people, this strategy is working to achieve our mission in a realistic way, by getting the people involved in ministry. Our people don't just sit back and listen to someone preach; they step out and make ministry tangible.

Volunteerism

Mobilizing a motivated volunteer army is critical to the success of any church. A long-established church that is in decline typically loses the "electricity" that makes for a vibrant congregation; thus, it struggles with getting people involved. The change agent must come in and jump-start involvement. It can be like pulling the cord on an old lawn mower that hadn't been started for several years. You pull and pull, but it doesn't start until after 150 attempts. Many pastors, feeling the pressure of keeping things running, act hastily and violate the principles that undermine volunteerism. Here are seven key principles in jump-starting your volunteer movement.

1. Take stock of your human resources.

You will not be able to mobilize your congregation over-night. You must ask yourself what percentage of your congregation you can realistically mobilize in a given year. You then must add up the number of volunteer positions you need to fill. Then ask yourself "Is this doable?" In most cases, there are more spots open than there are willing and able people to fill them.

2. Simplify until you can get your placement strategy on-line.

We were faced with the difficult task of simplifying our program menu without giving the perception that we were going backwards. The church needed an achievable, realistic goal. Avoid resurrecting programs that died during the declining years. Some will be eager to get those programs started again, but you need to be careful not to create an expectation you cannot fulfill. Remember that people get equally upset over a program not working as they do over not having one at all.

Another idea is to eliminate those programs that do not have leadership in place. You can also work on scaling back in those areas where there is duplication. Ideally, you eliminate those programs that are not contributing strategically to your mission statement or are not working any more. Motivate your people with the idea of doing one thing well versus two things poorly.

3. Make volunteering a part of your mission.

Our mission is to transform people, through the work of the Holy Spirit, into fully developing followers of Christ (see chapter 5). One of the key elements of a Christ follower is the emphasis on service or "making an impact with our lives." People at PBC have a sense that a life of service is critical to their spiritual development. People need to see that their volunteer investment is a part of God's plan in developing them, as well as contributing to the well-being of a group of people who make up their spiritual family.

4. Build your placement strategy around biblical principles.

The New Testament is extremely clear about the philosophy for mobilizing your people to service. The minister should use these passages to educate and develop a strategy. Here are two examples:

> It was he who gave some to be apostles, some to be prophets, some to be evangelists, and some to be pastors and teachers, to prepare God's people for works of service, so that the body of Christ may be built up until we all reach unity in the faith and in the knowledge of the Son of God and become mature, attaining the full measure of perfection found in Christ. . . . From him the whole body, joined and held together by every supporting ligament, grows and builds itself up in love, as each part does its work. (Eph. 4:11-13, 16)

> Therefore, I urge you, brothers, in view of God's mercy, to offer yourselves as living sacrifices, holy and pleasing to God, which is your spiritual worship. . . . Just as each of us has one body with many members, and these members do not all have the same function, so in Christ we who are many form one body, and each member belongs to all the others. We have different gifts, according to the grace given us. If a man's gift is prophesying, let him use it in proportion to his faith. If it is serving, let him serve; if it is teaching, let him teach; if it is encouraging, let him encourage; if it is contributing to the needs of others, let him give generously; if it is leadership, let him govern diligently; if it is in showing mercy, let him do it cheerfully. (Rom. 12:1, 4-8)

The basic principles that are taught in the Bible energize people toward meaningful involvement. God wants everyone to know that they are important and have a unique contribution to make. God has endowed each one with specific gifts and wants them to know that he brought them to the congregation for a purpose. God wants them to know that what they *do* for Christ is merely an overflow of who they *are* in Christ.

The role of the staff is to assist the members in discovering their unique design in Christ and their personal passions. The results of these assessments should be used to place a person in service.

5. Install a human resource department.

For years, the business world has understood the value of a special team in companies to help recruit, select, and place people correctly. The church lives or dies by volunteer involvement. It seems to make perfect sense to invest in a team that concentrates its full energy in mobilizing the body effectively. Most churches have some person who works on a human resource or personnel team that can get them started.

6. Identify your systems.

It is not enough to have a good philosophy. There are three critical elements to a successful human resource team.

- *You must have a human resource director.*

- *You must identify your assessment tool.* We use a simple interview process that identifies (1) whether a person is a manager, influencer, or contributor, (2) how they make decisions, (3) whether they like to work on projects or with people, and (4) whether they like to work alone or on a team. The interview also identifies how much time the person wants to volunteer and what time slots they have available to work.

- *You must develop a job description booklet of volunteer responsibilities.* This time-consuming process is critical to the success of a mass volunteer movement within a church. Many churches struggle to place people because they have not identified specific jobs they need filled. We have discovered that the majority have a "pull" in their makeup versus a "push." This means that most people wait to be pulled into a team to fulfill a specific role. Only a small portion of a congregation will actually push themselves into a role.

Here is an example of a volunteer job description that comes out of our Job Opportunities Booklet (J.O.B.).

Title	**Elders Prayer Card**
Department	Elders
Mission	To inform and encourage people in the body that the elders are praying for their specific requests
Manager	Rita Ballow
Design	C, S, C, T Level 1
Duties	To take the request that the elders prayed for and create a postcard that is mailed to the respective people
Time	1 - 2 hours per week
Place	Church office
Training	Microsoft Word processor experience helpful

This job description is self-explanatory except for the "Design" and "Level" categories. The Design includes letters that are simply codes to the kind of person that would be effective in this type of job. The first letter refers to one of three categories:

C = Contributor
M = Manager
I = Influencer

The second letter refers to one of two categories:

S = Self (likes to work by themselves)
T = Team (likes to work on a team)

The third letter refers to one of two categories:

O = Open (likes open-ended projects)

C = Closed (likes projects with quick completion or closure)

The fourth letter refers to one of two categories:

T = Things (likes to work with things)
P = People (likes to work with people)

The Elder Prayer Card job therefore is best filled by a person who is a Contributor (C), who likes to work by themselves (S), on a project that has closure (C).

The "Level" refers to the kind of maturity required for the position. There are three levels. Level 1 is an entry job that can be done by most members of the congregation. Level 2 is a job that requires a greater level of maturity but does not require membership. Level 3 is a job that requires an even greater level of maturity as well as church membership.

In 1992, we hired a woman in our congregation who has a background in psychology, counseling, and assessments. Her first assignment was to develop an accurate and simple curriculum based on an interview process. The name for this new program is *Incite*. We are discovering, along with an increasing number of other churches, that it is more effective to custom-make our own curricula based on the unique needs of our congregation rather than buy materials off the shelf. The person interested in serving within the church does some self-examination regarding a specific area in their past (i.e., work experience, hobbies) where they felt personally enriched and received satisfying results. They then meet with our human resource director or team for the interview. The department, through the use of a support staff, follows up on each person to make sure the placement into their chosen area actually took place.

Developing a strategy for effective volunteerism takes time, but it is worth it considering the alternative of ministerial burnout or slow progress. It is a process that may take two years before significant results are actually seen. However, after it is in place, you will thank God you did it! Here is what two people had to say about the positive impact their involvement has made in their life:

> When I was 15 years old I became a Christian and I also committed myself to ministry, however, my life went another direction and for years I did not even consider that commitment. But for the first time in about ten years that commitment seems very real to me and is one that I am taking seriously. I don't even know if you know all the things I am involved in because of the commitment I have made in the last year. God is doing great things through this church to bring about life change—I am one of those people. Thank you.

> Being able to be a part of a church that allows a member of the body to use their gifts is a true spiritual awareness. Through these experiences, I have expanded my knowledge of my worth and purpose, to God, myself, and others.

CHAPTER IX

A FRESH APPROACH
TO CHILDREN'S MINISTRY

COMEBACK CONCEPTS

1. A twentieth-century principle that will be carried into the twenty-first century is this: Parents will determine their church involvement largely by the satisfaction and visible growth of their children.

2. The church of the twenty-first century will move further away from the Sunday school format and curriculum to structures of children's celebration and small groups.

3. The church of the twenty-first century must have a plan to figure out how to make families spiritually healthier in their congregations.

Take a strong emphasis on contemporary Sunday services, vital community groups and small groups, mix it with a senior minister in his early thirties and a large city heavily populated with baby boomers, and what do you get? A growing children's ministry!

For several years, we operated with the traditional structure of age-graded Sunday school classes. Children came to the adult services once they reached the first grade. Under the direction of a dedicated part-time staff, we did everything we could to make this old paradigm look good. However, we knew we had to restructure this ministry for several good reasons:

1. It was a volunteer recruitment nightmare. Our Sunday morning children's ministry (birth to sixth grade with 450 in attendance each Sunday) took two hundred people to fully staff it.

2. Recruiting a large number of volunteers to prepare lessons and effectively teach them to children Sunday after Sunday was a mission without common sense. We knew there was only a small number of people in our congregation who were truly gifted to teach children. In a day when children are entertained with incredible special effects, you cannot afford to be an average teacher. Parents wanted to be involved with their children's spiritual development, but the weight of lesson preparation was discouraging to most. As a result we had some great teachers, but for the most part, we had guilt-ridden parents who couldn't say "no" under pressure.

3. We knew that a parent has the greatest influence on a child from birth to twelve years of age. After this the influence begins to shift to peers, youth leaders, coaches, teachers, and the like. All four of my children currently fall within the former age bracket. They would rather spend time with me and my wife than anyone in the entire world. We know that day is quickly coming to an end, so our strategy is to capitalize on the moment by spending as much time with them as we can. Our church leaders knew that an effective strategy would involve the right resources and would encourage parents to be the primary spiritual leaders in their children's life during this stage of their development.

4. The children lacked the celebration-size gathering mentioned earlier (see chapter 8 under "The Relationally Structured Church"). Their classroom format of fifteen to twenty-five children, the same structure they conform to all week in school, lacked the energy and vitality that can come from the uninhibited worship of little children. While our adult services have upbeat contemporary music, it is still designed for adults, not

children. We did not want our children to think of worship as merely a time to sit still and stay quiet while their parents listen to a man talk to them on an adult level. We wanted the children to fall in love with the God who calls us all his children.

5. Our children's staff was spending all its time recruiting volunteer teachers instead of focusing on the spiritual development of children. Under the traditional system, you do not need a children's specialist but a used car salesman. We realized this when most of the staff purchased mobile phones, which were plastered to their ears whenever you saw them, morning, noon, or night. We knew we had to change the old system to free these incredibly talented staff members to have their full impact on parents and children.

6. Children's curriculum is almost totally useless. However, in all fairness to the publishers, they have a difficult job of developing materials for halfhearted and ill-equipped parents. We do not envy their position. To add insult to injury, we discovered that our truly gifted teachers were not using the curriculum at all. Yet we spent thousands of dollars each year to stock our shelves with such curriculum. Each Sunday our children would bring home wads of meaningless paper that had been colored or had cotton balls glued to it. My goal as a parent, and embarrassingly as the pastor, was to get rid of this throwaway curriculum before we got home.

In 1990 I began to brainstorm with my board on creative ideas for the children's ministry. We came up with a good list of principles, most of which are mentioned earlier. With these helpful discussions in mind, I looked for feedback on our ideas from other pastors when I attended ministerial conferences. Most of them were in the same situation with very few new ideas being circulated. The average senior minister felt that the children's ministry was successful if the monkey was off his back and there wasn't much "grumbling" going on among the parishioners. However, we were too far into it to turn back. There had to be a better way.

I continued working with my children's staff. Most of our staff members and key volunteers were trained for the traditional public school classroom, which made it difficult initially to think beyond the classroom structure and curriculum. Finally, an idea emerged with three significant parts to it: The Children's Celebration, Special Projects and Events, and Family Night.

The Children's Celebration

For our Sunday morning program, we wanted to (1) reduce the number of teachers, (2) include an element of worship and celebration for a large group of children tailored to their needs, (3) involve parents as caregivers and coaches, (4) throw out the useless curriculum, and (5) maintain a small group dynamic.

Here's what we came up with. We would start with the first to sixth graders. If it worked, we would carry the concept down to the three-year-olds. The children meet in large rooms. First through third grades meet in one room and fourth through sixth grades meet in another. There are different themes for each section. These themes last for one year and then will be changed. For example, the first to third grade theme this year is "The Clubhouse," and the fourth to sixth grade theme is "The Big League." There are no chairs in this room; just big circle rugs that children gather around in groups of ten. There are ten to fifteen circle groups in each large room. These rooms are completely geared for children, not adults.

When a new child enters their appropriate room, they are welcomed by adult greeters who register them and give parents a brochure explaining our vision, values, and topics for the children's ministry at PBC. The child then goes to the assigned circle where he or she is greeted by nine other children who stay in that circle with the new arrival from week to week. Each circle group has a basket in it holding all the supplies and simple instructions necessary for the day's activities. We use a curriculum new to the industry.[1] They produce a quality hands-on curriculum without any throw-away papers.

Each circle group has two parents, a coach and assistant coach, who work with the ten children. There is no preparation work for the coaches. They begin to work with the children on a hands-on project that fits the theme for the day. About fifteen minutes into the seventy-minute program, the children's attention is drawn to the stage. One to two worship leaders lead the children in a high energy and active time of celebration. All the music tracks that are used are developed by a creative artist in our church who eagerly volunteers his time to tinker with the modern equipment in our sound studio.

After the time of celebration and worship, a gifted storyteller, called a Bible Explorer, delivers a ten- to twelve-minute message. These storytellers can draw on a number of creative teams who are "on call." These teams include drama, magicians, special games, puppets, science experiments, and the like. One of our teachers dresses in costume depending on the biblical character being portrayed. Some of these storytellers are parents, some are single people. What they have in common is a unique gift to teach children in such a way that it captivates the young hearts. Any church is truly blessed to have a small handful of these talented people.

Following the teaching time, the children turn back to their coaches for a time of application. The coach and assistant coach are given a few questions to ask the children to draw out some things that they can do to apply the day's theme. During this last stage of the meeting, the students also recite a memory verse as well as have a time of prayer.

Children are encouraged to invite other children to their circle group. Once a group reaches ten, however, another group is started. It is the responsibility of the coaches, along with the volunteer "manager" of each overall group, to sensitively decide how the new group will be formed. We have a goal that these children might sense a feeling of community among one another. Our staff encourages parents to do things with the families in their child's circle group (birthday parties, campouts, BBQs, and so on).

A good plan of communication minimizes resistance. Before this program was implemented in August of 1993, we knew it needed to be preceded with good communication to everyone in the church. We started by presenting the plan to the board. They were excited that the seeds of their ideas were growing into a workable and creative plan. We then communicated the master plan to the overall staff who worked out the detail effects this program would have on our other ministries and schedules. From this meeting a number of action steps were created in terms of budget allowances and room rearranging.

The most difficult step came in working with a children's ministry team that led our Sunday night AWANA Program. This ministry required ninety volunteers to keep it running. They had worked hard to keep the ministry alive for three years but were struggling. We felt we needed to put all our energies into doing the Sunday morning program well rather than trying to limp along with two weak programs. We knew that the AWANA leadership needed a break and could really impact the success of the morning program if they got behind it.

Instead of meeting with the entire AWANA team of volunteers, I started by meeting the director. She is one of our most talented and hardworking volunteers. I not only shared the vision with her but also offered her a paid part-time position with our children's staff to assist us in implementation of this new ministry. She accepted. I then proceeded to meet with the other six key leaders of the AWANA Program. After three meetings, we were able to secure their support. Here is a letter of one of those six key leaders:

> I am so thankful for your leadership and vision. As a marketing strategist, I appreciate the focus on core competencies and moving full steam ahead. I applaud your vision for our children's ministry. It's exciting. And thank you for including us at the ground level. The energy you spent to communicate so personally with the AWANA team will pay mighty dividends, I am sure.

I feel valued as a worker to be among the first to respond to the idea. I am behind you all the way. I look forward to investing my gifts in the Children's Ministry. Thanks again for making the tough decisions and helping us all make the most impact for Christ.

From here we communicated the changes with our broader leadership team at our monthly leadership meeting on Sunday afternoons. I shared the vision for forty-five minutes and immediately following this time, I met with all the children's ministry volunteers and entertained their questions. The children's ministry staff, including the AWANA director, stood with me to field responses. There was an unusually high level of support for this major shift in concepts.

My final stage of communication was to tell the congregation. We picked a strategic Sunday morning service and built an entire theme around the new ministry vision. I entitled my sermon, "Five Ways to Turn Your Children on to God." In this message, we explained our new strategy and the ways we wanted the parents and congregation to be involved.

From that point on, our four part-time staff members and a team of committed volunteers went to work on implementation. It is still too early to assess the actual long-term results of this concept; it will probably undergo several revisions. However, a commitment has already been made that no matter what happens, we are not going back to the old paradigm of Sunday school.

There are more details that can be shared about this concept, both in terms of what we are doing and where we would like it to go. On many occasions since we have made the change from the traditional Sunday school structure, I have received countless testimonies of parents excited about their child's renewed interest in church and most important, in God. Surprisingly, as large as our church is, I have only received one light complaint from a parent who missed the traditional format.

Special Projects and Events

The second major segment of our new children's ministry vision is special projects and events. We have three part-time staff members (nursery director, early childhood director, and elementary director) who run the Sunday Children's Celebration Hour. Our overall children's director is responsible for managing this creative team as well as overseeing the special projects and events.

Examples of special events are Junior Getaway Camp for fourth to sixth graders, bumper bowling for first to third graders, and a skating party on Sunday morning called Sunday Funday. Our goal is to create a greater sense of community and family within our church families.

An example of a special project comes from our children's drama ministry. A group of highly gifted volunteers with theater backgrounds works with about sixty kids three times a year to execute a Christian-based drama. This fall, they developed a project called "Short Stops." It is a story, which includes acting, music, props, and choreography, about a Little League team that was forced to make choices about relationships within the team. Children were recruited for everything—to assist in directing, running sound, and so on. At each practice, the children's drama director would lead the children in a time of sharing, praying, and worship. This play was done on four different occasions.

1. It was done for the parents.
2. It was done in pieces in the Sunday morning adult services for a series we did entitled "Eight Steps to Spiritual Fitness."
3. It was done for the rest of the children in our church.
4. It was done for three hundred inner-city children. Not only did our children perform the play for these children, but they also served them ice cream afterward. This concept has really helped our children to become "Serving Believers" (see chapter 5). At press time, the children are working on a Christmas drama entitled *The Gift Goes On*. We plan for

over five hundred inner-city children to attend this special project.

Family Night

One of the major principles we agreed about was to create within this new strategy a role for parents as the key influences in their child's life from birth to the sixth grade. We wanted to do something to strengthen the family. At a men's retreat in 1992, I asked a group of men to identify their major concern for their life. The overwhelming consensus: "We want to become the spiritual leaders of our homes."

From this finding and other discussions, we developed the third arm of our children's ministry vision. *We want families to commit to spending one night a week together.* God created the best small group ever—the family. We want to encourage families to take the primary role for developing their children.

Here is how Family Night works. A family in our church decides to make the commitment to develop a Family Night once a week by signing a Family Night Covenant form. The parent(s) receive a packet that explains how to organize themselves. The Family Night Covenant form gets put in our church database. Each month, our children's director sends out a Family Night Resource Letter, which contains ideas, anecdotes, resources, and stories from other families. This letter is sent only to those families who have made this one-year commitment. At the end of their commitment, they must sign another covenant form that ensures that they will continue receiving the Resource Letter for another year.

During our monthly meeting with our children's ministry volunteers, I introduced the Family Night idea in a most unusual way. One of my staff members saw a commercial on television from the Mormon Church for a concept they developed called *Family Home Evening.* They offered a free video, which we ordered. The video portrayed almost exactly what we wanted to do, and it was done very well.

We showed this entire video clip to our volunteers but stopped it short of the very end where the words "Church of Jesus Christ of Latter-day Saints" appears on the screen. I asked people what they thought of the idea. People had tears in their eyes. Everyone agreed this was a worthy goal. I then took the video off pause to reveal the source. The jaws across the room dropped. I then shared that the Mormon Church has been one of the fastest growing churches in America over the last twenty years and that some surmise that this growth is due to their emphasis on the family. I then shared that emphasis on the family is a good idea for us. We began this ministry in 1994 and believe we are heading in the right direction. We also have a sense that more effective strategies will be discovered. We want to stay open to how we can more effectively train children. For some reason, this change has been met with the least amount of resistance. We think it is because it works and the children love it. One man in the congregation put it well when he told me, "I don't know if I understand exactly the changes you have made, but all I know is that we used to drag our children to church; now they drag us."

CHAPTER X

FROM NIGHTMARES TO DREAMING

COMEBACK CONCEPTS
1. Once the revitalization process is complete, the change agent must work toward deepening and sustaining the new order.
2. The change agent must be able to look at what the next ten years will hold and begin preparing for it.

By 1994, four years had passed, and the revitalization process was done. The bleeding had stopped, and the wounds were healed. The congregation realized that the nightmares were over, and it was time for dreaming again. At one of our leadership rallies, we officially declared the comeback complete.
Respecting Organizational Cycles

Those first four years were intense, and the change has been necessarily great. The congregation has bravely weathered these changes. However, an organization must take a "time out" every three to five years to deepen the impact of the changes in the lives of the people. One of the difficult challenges for the change agent, who thrives on chaos and newness, is to realize that it is best for the organization to catch its breath.

Our board understands these inevitable cycles, which they have experienced in their own businesses. We have, conse-

Our board understands these inevitable cycles, which they have experienced in their own businesses. We have, consequently, laid out a basic fifteen-year plan that factors in the reality of these cycles.

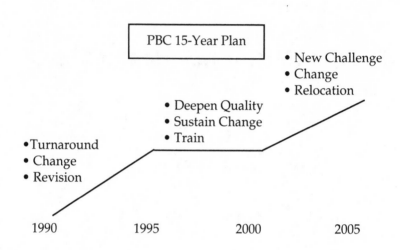

In the first five years, we changed just about everything to effectively position ourselves for a biblical mission and ministry for the twenty-first century. We completely changed the leadership structure, the worship service, the adult ministries, and the children's ministries. We redefined the members of our body as the real ministers; we built an entirely new staff team; we changed the way we place volunteers; we also eliminated many established programs that were no longer working or were too draining on our resources.

In the next five years, we must focus on deepening the ministry in the lives of our people. No organization can continue to stand the strain of the level of change we have introduced. We decided that we need to go into a management cycle to effectively install this new way of ministry. This means we are going to focus on training our people to function in this new strategy. Our people must be thoroughly equipped if our vision is ever to go beyond a nice document or sermon. We have a healthy number of new people coming into our church who want to become a part of us. We must develop new leaders and deepen the leaders we already have if we are ever going to include these new people into our biblical community and help them become fully developing followers of Christ. Our quality leadership base must be thickened and expanded.

By 2000, we believe our body will be prepared to enter another level of reaching our mission. It will be time to stretch our faith in a major way again. It will involve dynamic change and adjustment.

What is this new challenge? **We must reach out in greater and more effective ways to touch people's lives with Christ.**

Dreaming Bigger Dreams

Relocation: A dream to reach more unchurched people through strategic repositioning

Pantego Bible Church is sitting on seven acres of land in the central section of Arlington. This is a nice but older section of town. The city has grown from the north and currently toward the south. Both the north and south sides of Arlington have major east/west interstates running through them. Getting to our central location is rather difficult based on the way the city was built. This creates an obvious problem. The leadership summarizes this problem by saying, "We are a neighborhood church with a metroplex vision." While we have a growing number of people who work their way through the maze of streets to our facilities, we feel we are not ideally located for long-term growth. The central problem is not so much with the size of our facilities, but the location of our facilities. A more visible and accessible location will practically open up the entire Dallas/Fort Worth area to the spiritual service we have worked so hard to make effective for Christ.

To deal with this dilemma, the governing board decided to put together a long-range facilities planning task force. After four meetings, the task force presented a proposal to the board to put a contract on a twenty-acre plot of land on the north interstate. This land not only faces a major interstate, but it can be accessed easily by both exits on either side of it. Believe it or not, the cost of this prime real estate is only $225,000.

The board created a purchasing strategy that allows for the greatest amount of financial flexibility. Instead of the church purchasing the property, a group of business people in the church formed a limited partnership to buy the land. They will give the church the first option to purchase the property within the next three years. The obvious intent is for the church to purchase the property; however, if, in the next three years the church fails to sustain its current growth trend, then we could pass on the option to purchase the land, allowing the managing partner of the property to sell it and distribute the potential profits to the limited partners.

We sent a letter to the congregation explaining the above details. Many people are excited about being a part of such a grand vision. I admit that this decision puts "butterflies" in my stomach, but I know that we need to have the faith to position this positive church in a location that can reach more of the unchurched and disengaged people in the Dallas/Fort Worth metroplex. This is a dream for the future. As a matter of fact, our goal is to be sitting in our new Worship Center on the first Sunday of the year 2000.

Outreach: A dream to reach out to those outside of our church

A dream that we have as a church is to garner our strengths to make a significant difference beyond the people who will ever come to our church. We strongly believe, however, that the strategies for effective outreach for the future must be radically changed for the twenty-first century. For example, when it comes to overseas, cross-cultural missions, we must identify new strategies that account for the massive changes that have taken place in our world. We must look toward working through national leaders more and lose our preoccupation with sending American career missionaries as the goal. We must look at concentrating our resources as churches in fewer, more strategic places to make a deeper and more lasting difference as opposed to "bragging" about the number of missionaries we support for a hundred dollars a month. I believe that the "adopt-a-people group" movement will have a bright future on into the twenty-first century because it rallies a body and concentrates their financial, physical, emotional, and spiritual resources around a specific group of people in a specific geographical region.

Another component to our outreach dream is to become much more effective in reaching out to the broken, bruised, and abandoned in our own community. The evangelical church of the twenty-first century must take a serious look at the needs of its own community if it is to accomplish the biblical mandates found in the teachings of Jesus and if it is to maintain or obtain any credibility within its community for spiritual work.

Our dream, now that we have come back, is to take a greater role in outreach.

Church-based Seminary Training: A dream to participate in the training of a new generation of leaders to expand the work and to carry on the work after us

For the church to be effective on into the twenty-first century, more of the training of future pastors and church leaders will need to take place in a church. One of our dreams is to be involved in the resurrection of this old paradigm with some new, contemporary improvements. There are many issues to be addressed such as accreditation, cost, and the role of the existing seminaries. We have already taken several key steps to get us involved in this process. I believe that this process will take a very prominent role in the next ten years in the training of ministers.

Teaching Church: A dream to help other established churches come back from decline

We are dreaming about the way God can take our experience to help other churches in similar situations. I think the Teaching Church model, which has become more prominent in the last ten years, has something significant to offer the churches of the twenty-first century. There needs to be more such teaching churches. Our dream is to be a teaching church with a specialty of helping others develop comeback strategies.

Funding the Vision

No book could be complete without a discussion on how we paid for all of this. I'm not completely sure, but one thing I do know, faithful giving seems to follow big visions. We didn't use gimmicks, guilt, or promises of material success to get the money. These strategies have worked for some to produce cash, but I can't live with the results they produce in people's lives. We have treated giving more as a part of becoming a fully developing follower of Christ than as a need for our church to keep its doors open.

In 1989, our giving to the general fund was $370,796. Each year, for the last five years, we have experienced a 20 percent increase in giving to our general fund. If this trend continues, we will see our 1995 general fund giving reach close to one million dollars. The following sections outline eight specific things we have done and are implementing to increase our giving and fund the vision.

1. Increase revenues by decreasing expenses.

For the first few years, the injured church must operate on extremely limited funds. People hold back their giving to places that are showing signs of collapse. People will not start giving substantially again until they see signs of strength and stability. This means we had to make the most of every dollar we received. Here are two critical steps we took. First, we increased our financial resources by cutting back on costly programs that did not strategically advance our vision. Second, we increased our financial resources by making the staff and ministry leaders responsible for administrative budgets for their area. For example, we use copiers that require departmental codes to use them. Each time a staff member makes a copy, it is charged to his or her account. In the past, when staff members were preparing for a meeting for ten people, they would make fifteen copies just to make sure they were covered. Since this expense now comes out of their budget, they only make ten.

2. Create a task force to put together a one- to two-year plan for raising revenue.

The pastor of administration put together a task force of about seven people to prepare a practical plan for increasing our revenues. They each received a copy of Lyle Schaller's book *44 Ways to Expand the Financial Base of Your Congregation.*[1] The task force pulled out the ideas that would work best for our church. The six ideas that follow flowed from the recommendations of the task force.

3. Consider user fees.

One of the strategic ways a church can increase its productivity and cash flow is to charge user fees for certain services and products. In our experience, we have found that people will pay for extras they deem to hold value; they do not take such payments out of their giving fund. If a person pays ten dollars for a study book or a special event, he or she doesn't, for the most part, consider this a part of his or her giving plan. If we are asked why we are charging for a product or service, which seldom occurs, we simply explain that there is no money in the budget to provide this service or product, so in order to provide it, we must charge a fee.

We have received up to half a million dollars annually in user fees for such things as:

- Membership class notebooks
- Community Group Bible study guides
- Church directories
- Camps
- Youth events
- Cassette tapes
- Facility or vehicle rentals
- Biblical literacy class
- Seminars and conferences at the church

4. Develop a plan to teach your congregation about stewardship at strategic times.

We wanted to ensure that people understood the biblical concepts behind giving because it is such a dynamic part of Christian development. We also recognized that many people cannot give—not because they don't want to, but because they mismanage their money, leaving nothing left over to give. This called for stewardship and financial management classes taught from a biblical perspective.

Our membership class is the first place we introduce and teach on the concept of biblical stewardship. It is also an item we ask prospective new members to evaluate on their Spiritual Fitness Plan. (See Appendix A for a copy of the Spiritual Fitness Plan.) If they mark stewardship as one of their lowest areas spiritually, we recommend that they take the "Master Your Money" course.[2]

We offer this course several times a year, and it is open to the entire congregation. It is taught by financial professionals within our congregation who personally practice the principles they teach. A follow-up computer class is offered for those who want to learn how to use a computer-based financial management program.

5. Consider using stewardship cards.

The task force also recommended using stewardship cards. We knew the congregation would understand our desire to plan as a church. If they indicated to us their giving plans, it would assist us in this process.

We also have three major funds. We ask members and regular attendees to give to our General Fund, Missions Fund, and Building and Property Fund. If they indicate to us one time on the Stewardship Card how they want their money divided among these funds, our computer system automatically divides their actual giving according to those percentages without their having to indicate on their checks how much goes to each fund each time.

The primary goal behind using stewardship cards is to encourage planning. If a person plans to give, there is a greater chance he or she will give. The stewardship drive, as in most churches, begins in November and goes through January. Some people do not turn in their cards, but we feel that this process is helping many people become more consistent givers.

6. Mail giving envelopes to your congregation monthly.

The Southern Baptists have been doing it for years and have experienced success. A friend of mine who is a Southern Baptist senior minister indicated that giving will increase up to 19 percent if a church mails out giving envelopes on a monthly basis. After talking to some of our people about the idea, we decided that it could be a helpful reminder and system for our people. We pay an outside service to mail the envelopes. We simply give them an updated list each month from our data base. While we are not sure that this one move is responsible for our 10 to 20 percent increase in giving over the last five years, we feel that it has contributed to the success.

7. Mail a quarterly giving statement that records giving against goals.

Another idea that we implemented is to mail quarterly giving statements to our people. These statements report their actual giving against the goal they set on their stewardship card. The IRS is requiring actual statements versus simply validating your giving through canceled checks, so this process was well received by the church members. On many occasions, members have sent us additional gifts to make up for one or more times they missed in the previous quarter, along with notes to thank us for providing this service.

8. Organize one to two simple fund drives that tap into your people's accumulated funds.

Most people in our church give out of their weekly, bi-monthly, or monthly income checks. There is another source that is sometimes overlooked—accumulated funds such as savings accounts. By identifying legitimate needs to the congregation several weeks before the drive and by providing special envelopes, we have increased our giving by up to $200,000 a year.

Other churches are far more sophisticated than PBC in this area. There is more we can learn from these churches. However, we feel that we have developed a healthy strategy to raise the funds we need without making money the central mission. Our strategy has enabled us not to get sidetracked from effective ministry.

Final Words

For the first time in my five years at PBC, I feel that my faith and courage is being challenged to the limits. I cannot believe we have made so much progress. However, I know these steps are right and necessary. I do not believe that the feeling of fear necessarily means that the direction you are heading is wrong. I also know the future will require exceptional leadership skills. As the senior minister, I am called to be one of the individuals to exhibit those skills. My focus must be on God's lead and timing. I don't want this to be the building of my little kingdom; it's God's big kingdom! In the early days, selfish ambitions never crossed my mind. Now that the church has recovered with a new vision, such personal gratification is a subtle temptation to any leader. I need a reality check every week. Each Monday when I come into the office, I bow my head before God to make sure that I am not holding too tightly to PBC. This is Christ's church. I am only a servant, an under shepherd. As God continues to provide the increase to our church, I pray that I do not lose this perspective. Many churches have grown into the thousands while the senior minister's life and ministry were systematically unraveling. I want to finish the race faithfully.

The process of revitalization comes to an end when the church recovers, but the process of revisioning does not. One thing our church has learned for sure is that it doesn't matter how strong you are today; if you lose your vision for the future, you will surely decline. The church of Jesus Christ must stay dynamic and alive in order to stay effective. The intensity of focus and work must continue at Pantego Bible Church and at your church as well.

APPENDIX A

Spiritual Fitness Plan

Name _____   Date   _____

Address _____   Home Phone _____

City _____ Zip _____   Work Phone _____

Consultant_____

SPIRITUAL HISTORY

Church Background

    Type of church, if any, previously attended _____

    Date last attended   _____

    Date you started attending PBC   _____

    Community Group   _____

    Growth Group   _____

Personal Background

    Outside activities—previous or current volunteer involvement

_____

APPENDIX A

PERSONAL STATUS

Single _____ Married _____ Divorced_____

Remarried _____ Single Parent _____ Widowed_____

Blended Family ____

Ages of Children ____ ____ ____ ____ ____ ____

PERSONAL ASSESSMENT	*low*					*high*
Corporate Worship Attendance	1	2	3	4	5	6
Personal Worship/Prayer	1	2	3	4	5	6
Lifestyle of Worship	1	2	3	4	5	6
Quality Relationships with						
Other Christians	1	2	3	4	5	6
Knowledge of God's Word	1	2	3	4	5	6
Personal Study of God's Word	1	2	3	4	5	6
Marriage Relationship	1	2	3	4	5	6
Relationship with Children	1	2	3	4	5	6
Physical Wellness	1	2	3	4	5	6
Job Satisfaction	1	2	3	4	5	6
Understanding of Gifts	1	2	3	4	5	6
Ministry Involvement	1	2	3	4	5	6
Giving	1	2	3	4	5	6
Sharing Your Faith with Others	1	2	3	4	5	6
Have You Been Baptized?						
(since becoming a Christian)	1	2	3	4	5	6

Spiritual Fitness Action Plan

Name _____ *Home Phone* _____ *Work Phone* _____

PERSONAL

1. Goal _____
   Action Step _____
2. Goal _____
   Action Step _____
3. Goal _____
   Action Step _____
4. Goal _____
   Action Step _____

FAMILY

1. Goal _____
   Action Step _____
1. Goal _____
   Action Step _____
1. Goal _____
   Action Step _____
1. Goal _____
   Action Step _____

■ *YES, I would like a follow-up call in one month.*

APPENDIX B

Spiritual Fitness Resource Card

WORSHIPING BELIEVER

- ♦ Baptism
  - Baptism in Worship Service as Public Testimony
- ♦ Corporate Worship
  - Worship Services
  - Children's Celebration Hour
- ♦ Personal Worship/Prayer
  - 201-*Personal Worship Workshop****
- ♦ Lifestyle of Worship
  - 202-*Life Vision* Centering Your Life Around God

GROWING BELIEVER

- ♦ Quality Relationships with other Christians
  - Growth Groups
  - Men's Integrity Groups
  - Creative Homemaker Groups
  - Youth Discipleship Groups
  - Children's Circle Groups

♦ Knowledge of God's Word   -   301-*Biblical Literacy*
Bible Basics
- 302-*Biblical Literacy*
10 Major Bible Themes*
(prerequisite: 301)

♦ Personal Study of God's Word -   Community Groups/
Personal Bible Study Plan
- Ladies' Bible Study

♦ Marriage Relationship   -   304-*Two to One*
Pre-Marital Class
- 305-*Family Life Conference*
Marriage Enrichment
- 306-*Annual Marriage Check-up*
- 307-*Discovering Your Mate's Design Workshop***

♦ Relationship with Children   -   308-*Family Life Conference*
Parenting Seminar
- 309-*Discovering Your Child's Design Workshop*
- Pantego Christian Academy K-12

♦ Physical Wellness   -   Aerobic Classes
- Adult Intramural Sports

♦ Job Satisfaction   -   311-*Job Fit Assessment*
- 202-*Life Vision*

SERVING BELIEVER

♦ Understanding of Gifts/   -   401-*INCITE*
Ministry Involvement
- 402-*Individual Operating Style (IOS) Assessment*
(prerequisite: 401 INCITE Orientation)

- 403-*Motif Advanced*
  Assessment
  (prerequisite: 401 INCITE
  Orientation)

♦ Giving
- 404-*Biblical Financial*
  Management Workshop
- PBC Giving/Stewardship
  Packet & Envelopes

♦ Sharing Your Faith
with Others
- 405-*How to Share Your Faith*
  Workshop***

*   **Beginning winter 1994**
**   **Beginning spring 1994**
*** **Beginning date to be determined**

APPENDIX C

STAFFING CHART

ELDERS
(9)

SENIOR PASTOR
(Full-time)
Support Staff (Part-time)

Team # 1: Worshiping Believer
Team Leader: Associate Pastor of Programming (Full-time)

Worship Leader (Full-time)
Assimilation/Membership (Part-time)
Publications/Media (Full-time)
Special Events (Part-time)
Support Staff (Full-time)

Win

Team # 2: Growing Believer
Team Leader: Associate Pastor of Adult Ministries (Full-time)

• Children's Minister (Part-time)
  Nursery Director (Part-time)
  Early Childhood Director (Part-time)
  Elementary Director (Part-time)
  Support Staff (Part-time)
• Associate Pastor of Student
  Ministries (FT)
  Assistant Pastor of Jr. High (Full-time)
  Youth Interns (Part-time)
  Assistant Pastor of College (Full-time)
  Support Staff (Part-time)
• Women's Minister (Part-time)
• Support Staff (Full-time)

Build

Team # 3: Serving Believer
Team Leader: Associate Pastor of Administration (Full-time)

• Director of Volunteer Placement (Part-time)
• Assistant Pastor of Missions (Part-time)
  Hispanic Pastor (Full-time)
  Support Staff (Part-time)
• Director of Finance (Full-time)
• Facilities Supervisor (Full-time)
  Custodians & Maintenance Crew
  Facilities Coordinator (Part-time)
• Support Staff (Full-time)
• Receptionist (Full-time)

Send

NOTES

1. New Wine into Old Wineskins

1. Lyle E. Schaller, *Strategies for Change* (Nashville: Abingdon Press, 1972), pp. 72-73.
2. Ralph Neighbour, *Where Do We Go from Here?* (Houston: Touch Publications, 1990), pp. 91-92.
3. Schaller, *Strategies for Change*, p. 77.
4. Ibid., p. 76.
5. Win Arn, *The Pastor's Manual for Effective Ministry* (Monrovia: Church Growth, Inc., 1988), p. 16.
6. George G. Hunter III, *How to Reach Secular People* (Nashville: Abingdon Press, 1992), p. 41.
7. Kenneth L. Woodward, "The Rites of Americans," *Newsweek*, November 29, 1993, p. 80.

3. Change Requires a Change Agent

1. Lyle E. Schaller, *Create Your Own Future!* (Nashville: Abingdon Press, 1991), p. 24.
2. Lyle E. Schaller, *Getting Things Done* (Nashville: Abingdon Press, 1986), p. 68.
3. *Personal Profile System®* (Minneapolis: Carlson Learning Company, 1977), p. 17. Reprinted with permission of Carlson Learning Company, Minneapolis, Minnesota.
4. Carlson Learning Company, p. 17.

4. The Magna Charta

1. Schaller, *Strategies for Change*, pp. 58-60.
2. Ibid., p. 58.

5. The Mission: From Believer to Disciple

1. Peter Drucker, "The Church in the 21st Century: New Tools for the New Paradigm," Leadership Network address, opening General Sess., Tyler, 19 Aug. 1991.
2. Peter Drucker, "Managing for Results: Meeting the Challenge of Accountability," Drucker Foundation Conference, Washington, D.C., 8-9 Nov. 1993.
3. Lyle E. Schaller, *The Seven-Day-a-Week Church* (Nashville: Abingdon Press, 1992), pp. 67-68.

8. Preparing for the Twenty-first Century

1. Joel Barker, *Discovering the Future: The Business of Paradigms* (Lake Elmo: ILI Press, 1989), p. 25.
2. Peter M. Senge, *The Fifth Discipline: The Art and Practice of the Learning Organization* (New York: Doubleday, 1990), pp. 5-11.
3. Lyle Schaller, *The Senior Minister* (Nashville: Abingdon Press, 1988), p. 100.
4. C. Peter Wagner, *Your Church Can Grow* (Ventura: Regal Books, 1965), pp. 111-26.

9. A Fresh Approach to Children's Ministry

1. For more information on "Group" educational materials, call 1-800-447-1070.

10. From Nightmares to Dreaming

1. Lyle E. Schaller, *44 Ways to Expand the Financial Base of Your Congregation* (Nashville: Abingdon Press, 1989).
2. Ron Blue, *Master Your Money Series* (Nashville: Thomas Nelson Publishers, 1991).